W9-CCO-988

This book belongs to

_____

a young woman
who loves God.

A Young Woman After God's Own Heart

A Devotional

Elizabeth George

HARVEST HOUSE PUBLISHERS
EUGENE, OREGON

Unless otherwise indicated, all Scripture quotations are taken from the HOLY BIBLE, NEW INTERNATIONAL VERSION®. NIV®. Copyright © 1973, 1978, 1984 by the International Bible Society. Used by permission of Zondervan. All rights reserved.

Material for devotions adapted from:

A Young Woman's Walk with God by Elizabeth George, Copyright © 2006
A Young Woman's Call to Prayer by Elizabeth George, Copyright © 2005
A Young Woman After God's Own Heart by Elizabeth George, Copyright © 2003

Every effort has been made to give proper credit for all stories, poems, and quotations. If for any reason proper credit has not been given, please notify the author or publisher and proper notation will be given on future printing.

Italics in scriptures indicate author's emphasis.

Cover photos © Photodisc

Cover by Dugan Design Group, Bloomington, Minnesota

A YOUNG WOMAN AFTER GOD'S OWN HEART—A DEVOTIONAL
Copyright © 2008 by Elizabeth George
Published by Harvest House Publishers
Eugene, Oregon 97402
www.harvesthousepublishers.com

Library of Congress Cataloging-in-Publication Data
    George, Elizabeth
    A young woman after God's own heart : a devotional / Elizabeth George.
        p. cm.
    ISBN 978-0-7369-2297-5 (pbk.)
    ISBN 978-0-7369-3089-5 (eBook)
    1. Teenage girls—Prayers and devotions. 2. Christian teenagers—Prayers and devotions. 3. Devotional calendars. I. Title.
    BV4551.3.G462 2008
    242'.633—dc22
                                                            2007034932

All rights reserved. No part of this publication may be reproduced, stored in a retrieval system, or transmitted in any form or by any means—electronic, mechanical, digital, photocopy, recording, or any other—except for brief quotations in printed reviews, without the prior permission of the publisher.

Printed in China

14 15 16 / RDS-SK / 12 11 10 9

Dear Friend,

As you begin this practical and fun book of devotions, I want to thank you. Because of you, and the many letters I've received from other young women who want to meet with God regularly, this book was born. Although it is small in size, its message is a big one—keep on seeking the Lord and loving Him with all your heart. These devotions are for you. On each page you'll find—

- life-changing truths from God's Word to your heart
- something to do each day to grow more like Jesus
- a prayer to help you talk to God about your life

Enjoy your journey into loving God even more!

With all my heart,

Elizabeth

1

Enjoy Jesus

Have you ever felt nervous…fidgety…on edge…cranky? And even though you didn't want to act the way you were, you kept on stomping through your day, lashing out at everybody who crossed your path? Well, take heart! You're not alone! This happened to Martha, a woman in the Bible. She got too involved in the activities of her life. In all her busyness, Martha didn't take time to enjoy Jesus and worship Him when He came to visit.

Are you thinking, *I would never ignore Jesus if He came to my house!* But imagine how easy it is to go about your day without lifting up a prayer, without doing devotions, without serving Jesus, without thanking Him. You're missing out! Put aside the busyness and chaos of school, pressures, and worries. Totally enjoy time with the Lord.

What can you say no to today so you can say yes to time with God?

Lord, I love You. I want to hang out
with You. Life gets crazy sometimes.
I want the peace of Your love. I want the joy
of being in Your presence. Amen.

2

A Heart After God

God is always looking for a heart that will obey Him, that will do His will. Do these words describe your heart? Is God's desire your desire? Do you follow hard after God—close to Him, on His heels, clinging to Him? If any behavior is keeping you from pursuing God with your whole heart, confess it, cast it off, and step right back onto God's path of peace and joy. Spend time in God's Word every day so you'll grow to better understand His character. Are there people in your life who have this kind of passion for God? Ask them how they keep their hearts focused on God.

As you desire all that God desires, love all that He loves, and humble yourself before Him, your heart will indeed become a heart after His. What a terrific thought! What a terrific life!

Jesus, I want a heart that abides in You.
Help me embrace Your desires rather than my
own. When I walk forward, I want to be headed
in the direction of Your heart. Amen.

3

Pitiful or Prayerful?

Attitude has to do with your moods. And your moods can be right and godly or they can be sinful. Is your attitude generally cheerful, helpful, vibrant, pleasant, positive, giving, respectful? Or do you tend to mope around, grunt and grumble, resent your parents, your family, your responsibilities…even your life as a teenager? Do you bring others down? Do you let others change your good mood into boredom, anger, or jealousy?

An upbeat, positive attitude is born, grown, and cared for in your quiet time as God's Word fills your heart and sets the path for your day. God points the way, and your prayer joins your heart with His. If you fail to have this all-important time with God, you're starting your day in weakness. Prayer changes all pitiful moods. It also changes a day with no plan to one of purpose.

*God, my moods shift quite a bit during a day.
I let the words and actions of others affect how
I think and feel. Give me Your heart and
perspective and attitude! Amen.*

Lots of Good

In Galatians 6:10 the apostle Paul said, "As we have opportunity, let us do good to all people, especially to those who belong to the family of believers." Begin working on goodness and then stand back as God grows in you a heart that serves. The instructions are simple. However, doing it takes a lifetime! John Wesley said,

> Do all the good you can,
> by all the means you can,
> in all the ways you can,
> in all the places you can,
> at all the times you can,
> to all the people you can,
> as long as ever you can.

There is so much good to be done. Once you start serving God by serving others, life gets exciting! Discover your heart of goodness and put it into action.

Lord, help me see the need for goodness all around me. I want my heart, hands, words, and deeds to serve You. Show me how, and give me a heart of true compassion. Amen.

5

Refocus Your Faith

If you aren't careful you can spend all day—and all night—doing less-important tasks—anything!—to put off the most difficult, but most rewarding "task" of all—praying. Why is it so hard to pray? Well, for one thing…you live in the world. The world affects you more than you think. It bombards you with encouragement to sin or distracts you from the things of God. Do you ever become so busy you forget to pray? To reflect? To take time to consider the decisions you are making?

Very few voices in the world encourage you to take care of spiritual things. And prayer is a spiritual exercise. It cuts through the busyness and refocuses your eyes, heart, mind, and full attention back on God. So take charge and pray!

God, the world can be pretty interesting and enticing. When my thoughts are more about clothes, friends, music, movies, and money than about faith, help me get my eyes back on You through prayer. Amen.

6

One Choice

Mary (Martha and Lazarus' sister) was a friend to Jesus and a woman whose heart was devoted to Him. She was preoccupied with one thing at all times—Jesus! Mary consistently made the choice to spend time hearing God through His Word and worshiping Him in her heart. She chose to spend some of her precious time with her wonderful and loving Lord. Time spent this way is never wasted, and the benefits can never be taken away from you. Why? Because it is time spent in activities that result in daily and everlasting blessings.

How do you spend your time with Jesus? Do you listen to Him with great attention? Do you bring your faults to His feet and ask for forgiveness? Do you thank Him for His forever friendship? Choose to invest your whole self in the time you spend with your Savior.

I love You, Jesus. I'm sorry for the times
when I don't talk to You with honesty,
openness, and respect. Today I give You
my heart and my love. Amen.

Wherever You Are

Every woman of wisdom works at creating a pleasant atmosphere in her space, her own little home-sweet-home. As a single woman, that home is wherever you happen to live. Whether you are in your own room in your parents' house or share it with a sister or two, whether you live in an apartment or a dorm room, the place or space you stay in is yours to "build." And the habits you develop now will help you down the road. Do you make your space inviting? Does it reflect your faith?

What you are at home is what you are. So are you messy or neat? Buried under things or on top of them? Unorganized or orderly? Living in chaos or following a plan? What character qualities are you showing as you care for your place, for your space? Your heart is showing. Do you need to make any changes?

Lord, I want my surroundings to show others my love for You. Help me develop a heart of discipline so that my space will be a delightful place to spend time with You and dream about what lies ahead. Amen.

THE HEART OF THE MATTER

God's Word on the Fruit of the Spirit

The word "fruit" is used in the Bible to refer to telltale evidence of what is on the inside of a person. If what's inside is good, the fruit of that person's life will be good. But what if what's inside is rotten? The fruit of that person's life will be bad. That's what Jesus taught when He said, "The good man brings good things out of the good stored up in him, and the evil man brings evil things out of the evil stored up in him" (Matthew 12:35).

What sort of fruit have you seen in your actions lately?

Any person who has received Jesus as Savior and Lord and has Christ living within will bear good fruit. She will be "filled with the fruit of righteousness that comes through Jesus Christ—to the glory and praise of God" (Philippians 1:11). How do you think exhibiting the fruit of righteousness brings glory and praise to God? And in what ways has your fruit shown others what Jesus is like?

In Galatians 5:22-23 the apostle Paul lists these godly habits—"the fruit of the Spirit is love, joy, peace, patience, kindness, goodness, faithfulness, gentleness and self-control." All nine fruit stand together and make up your walk with God. They are like a string of Christmas lights—with many lights that all light up at once when plugged into the electrical socket. But if one bulb goes out, the entire string goes out. That's how God's fruit is borne in your life. Not one of them can be missing, and all must be evident—be lit up— to be God's fruit.

As you recall your actions this week and today, were any of these spiritual habits missing? What must you do to get plugged into God, the ultimate power source, again?

8

Golden Rules

Do you put the lid back on the toothpaste tube? Believe it or not, this relates to your spiritual growth! How well you respect and get along with the people you live with and the way you live matters. Follow these "Golden Rules for Living."

> If you open it, close it.
> If you turn it on, turn it off.
> If you unlock it, lock it up.
> If you break it, admit it.
> If you can't fix it, call in someone who can.
> If you borrow it, return it.
> If you value it, take care of it.
> If you make a mess, clean it up.
> If you move it, put it back.
> If it belongs to someone else,
> get permission to use it.

The small, positive steps in life add up to better, more godly living.

Jesus, help me be courteous, thoughtful, and conscientious. When I neglect basic manners at home let me know and give me a heart to serve the people closest to me. Amen.

Step into the Quiet

What is your quiet time with God like? This is the question Dawson Trotman, founder of The Navigators ministry organization, asked young men and women applying for an overseas mission. Sadly, only one person out of 29 interviewed said her devotional life was a constant in her life, a source of strength, guidance, and refreshment.

How would an interview about your devotional life go? What answers would you give? If your answers aren't all that great, what can you do right this minute to set your life in a new direction that will ensure that you grow in your love for God's Word? "Every journey begins with a single step." And that includes your journey to becoming a woman after God's own heart!

Lord, I want to spend time with You.
I want to embrace a radical new way of
living that reflects Your heart and changes my
life from the inside out. Help me. Amen.

No Need to Panic

What would you do in an emergency? In a disaster? I had the opportunity to find out when a killer earthquake struck our home in California. It was early in the morning, and I was home alone when the ground began to buckle and crack beneath my bare feet. I panicked as I raced for the door. Then Psalm 46:1-2—verses I had memorized—came into my heart, "God is our refuge and strength, an ever-present help in trouble. Therefore we will not fear, though the earth give way and the mountains fall into the heart of the sea, though its waters roar and foam and the mountains quake with their surging." Sounds like an earthquake to me! I felt God's presence immediately.

Jesus tells us not to panic but to pray instead. If you spend time bringing your daily questions and worries to God, you'll be prepared to rest in His strength when the things around you shake, shudder, and quake.

Lord, there are times when I get scared.
My heart races, I feel confused, and I don't know
which way to turn. Remind me to turn to You
and Your strength! Amen.

Friends Forever

Do you make time for your friends? Do you talk on the phone, email, send notes? These practices build relationships, don't they? Do you make time for God too? Do you pause to talk to God, to listen for His leading, to read His love notes to you that are found in the Bible? When you do, you're developing the most important relationship in your life!

A high school pastor talked to his youth group about spending time with God. He asked, "Would you be willing to go on a bit of a fast each day…a time fast? Would you be willing to say no to time watching TV, no to time on the phone, no to time with friends, no to time in the mall to say yes to time with God?" How would you answer?

When you say yes to time with God, you are saying yes to a friend for life!

Lord, as much as I love my friends,
I'm so thankful You are more than a friend.
You are my heavenly Father, my Lord, and the
One I want to say yes to each day. Amen.

The Way to Your Dreams

When you choose God's ways you are reaching for His absolute best for you. Proverbs 3:6—"In all your ways acknowledge him, and he will make your paths straight"—could be your theme verse for life! This well-loved verse describes a two-step partnership with God. Your part is to stop and consult God along the way. God's part is to direct your paths and make them straight. This means you talk with God about every decision, word, thought, and response. *Whew!* It does get easier once you make this a habit!

Before you move ahead or before you react to someone or something, stop and pray first. Ask, "God, what would You have me do…or think…or say here?" And God will answer! He'll lead you to the dreams He has for you! Hallelujah!

Lord, help me notice all You're doing
in my life so I don't miss Your directions and
Your dreams for me. I can't wait to see where
your path leads! Amen.

Share in Prayer

Do you share the gift of prayer? The habit of praying is born and developed in private. But praying with others expands your prayer life. Do you know some sisters in Christ who share your heart for prayer? Maybe you can establish a prayer group with them. Are you shy about praying out loud? That's okay. A prayer group can be a gathering of committed friends who discuss their prayer concerns, pray silently for one another as a group, and then promise to pray for each other during the week. But, in time, I encourage you to pray for one another out loud. The more you pray aloud, the more comfortable you'll become in this area.

Whether you meet at a church, in homes, at school, or even in a park, be sure you actually pray when you get together. Answer God's call to prayer as an individual—and as a team.

Lord, I'd love to have a group of friends to pray with. Help me have the courage to suggest the idea to a few Christian friends. I can't wait to share my passion for prayer with others. Amen.

The Embrace of Grace

Name one practice in your life that you know is not pleasing to God. Do you have a habit that goes against His Word? Do you do something that is unhealthy or harmful to you or others? Put that specific act at the top of your prayer list. Then pray about it—every day. Pray about it every minute of every day if you have to. And confess it to God if you stumble. Ask Him to help you create a plan of action to radically remove this sin area from your life.

Even what seems like a small problem can be very tough to shake, especially if you have friends who encourage the practice or if you can't imagine what life would be like without that activity. Maybe you swear or you put others down. Maybe you struggle with boyfriends and temptation. No matter what it is, God won't ignore you. He won't turn you away or keep you from His embrace and His grace. You're not alone in this. He is with you!

God, I've been holding on to some sins.
I can't break from them on my own. I need
Your strength and help. Thank You for never
turning away from me. Amen.

Have you had a wake-up call in your life? (And I'm not talking about your alarm clock!) Well, I definitely did. One morning a woman called to invite me to speak at her church. As she talked, I thought, *Sure! I'll come!* Then, at about eight o'clock that night, the phone rang again. It was another woman asking me to speak at an event. As she provided details, I was shaking my head and already answering her in my mind: *No way!*

The next day I sat before the Lord and wondered, *Why was my response so different? Each event was a wonderful opportunity for ministry.* I realized I wasn't making spiritual decisions—I was making physical decisions. If I felt good, the answer was yes. If I didn't feel good or was tired, the answer was no.

Right then I made a commitment: "No decision made without prayer!" To seal the deal I turned to a blank page in my prayer notebook and wrote at the top, "Decisions to Make." I keep this list updated and refer to it every day. This prayer principle has helped me find God's will and has guided my life from that day on. Why don't you try it?

In Him,

Elizabeth

15

Being Seen

It isn't often that you see the large strong roots of a tree or the delicate roots of a flower because they're underground of course! This is where they receive their nourishment to grow and thrive. As great as it is to be with friends and family, in your life it's also important to step away from others once in a while. Drop out of your friends' sight for a bit of each day. Detour away from distractions such as TV, the phone, and the Internet. Why? So you can take care of your private life. So you can grow your hidden life. So you can nourish the secret life you enjoy with God.

When you're faithful to do this one thing each and every day, Wow! What a difference it makes. Go underground for awhile...and you'll be seen, heard, and fed by the One who created you.

Lord, I love to be around friends. It's fun to share
about my life, my interests, and my thoughts.
And I can share with You in the same way.
I can't wait to go underground and be seen
and heard just by You. Amen.

Lucky Girl

Faith isn't about luck. It's about love and relationship with God. However, you can count yourself as one lucky girl because you have the privilege of prayer. Just think about it. You can have an ongoing conversation with God Himself! The Creator of the universe listens to you and considers everything you say important.

May your heart always be encouraged to pray. And may your prayers always be lifted to your great God so that...

> you are growing in faith,
> you are handing off your problems,
> you are aware of the presence of God,
> you are less likely to panic when
>   troubles arise,
> you are changed and transformed into
>   the image of God's dear Son and your
>   Savior, Jesus Christ!

Heavenly Father, thank You for listening to me. So often I feel invisible or too intimidated to share with people around me. But I have You! Amen.

Just Like You

There's a young woman in the Bible who might be a lot like you. She's Mary, who became the mother of our Lord Jesus Christ. Maybe you already know that Mary was about 14 years old when God sent His angel Gabriel to speak to her. What else do we know about Mary at this point in her life? She was committed to God's will, she was favored by God, she was a virgin, and she was a young woman of prayer! In fact, her prayer life was so stunning that God used her—a teenager!—to teach Christian women how to pray. In what is called "The Song of Mary," the first thing Mary says is, "My soul glorifies the Lord and my spirit rejoices in God my Savior" (Luke 1:46). Can you feel the passion and the deep connection she has with the Lord?

Be inspired by Mary. She faced trials, fears, and uncertain times. Yet she held on to her faith and her prayer life, and God brought her through to do magnificent things. Just like you, Mary was a young woman after God's own heart.

Lord, I glorify You and rejoice in You.
You're my Savior! Thank You for the example of
Mary's prayer life and the amazing love she had for
You. I love You too. Please use me. Amen.

24/7 Relationship Help

Even the best relationships hit rocky points, right? It would be nice to have a 24/7 connection to a relationship expert. But wait a minute! You do! God does relationships big time. When you pray, you change the way you relate to everyone. That's because you can't think about yourself and others at the same time. Praying turns your attention to others. You also can't hate the person you're praying for because prayer is an act of love and it changes your heart. And you can't ignore the person you're praying for because when you lift up a friend, a brother or sister, a parent, or even an annoying classmate to God, that person is obviously on your mind. Do you see how a relationship problem can flip in the speed of prayer?

What relationships do you want to pray over today? Plan on amazing things happening!

Lord, my family and friends get on my nerves. Instead of getting angry or tuning them out, help me focus my attention on them when I pray. Some of my relationships need radical change! Change my heart and the relationships in my life. Amen.

What's Hot, What's Not

Quick! Take your temperature! No, not to see if you have a fever, but to see if you're spiritually hot. God has a few things to say to you in Revelation 3:15-16 about your heart temperature: "I know your deeds, that you are neither cold nor hot. I wish you were either one or the other! So, because you are lukewarm—neither hot nor cold—I am about to spit you out of my mouth." (You can certainly tell what temperature God wants your heart to be!)

To be coldhearted means to be unemotional, to be unaware of God. And to be lukewarm means to be indifferent. Imagine being cool toward God. But as a woman of faith, you're to be hot-hearted—passionate, committed, excited, and blazing with love for God. And the world will know it because everyone sees the light and feels the heat of a heart on fire for God.

Lord, I want to be passionate for You and about You. When I start to cool down, set my spirit on fire. I want my mood, my actions, and my attitude to spark flames of faith everywhere I go. Amen.

The Best Prayer

Is God your everything? Do you bring your troubles, your dreams, and your hopes to Him? If not, is it because you still need to receive Jesus Christ as your Savior? Why not begin an exciting journey with God? I encourage you to say the best prayer of all:

> God, I want to be Your child, a true
> woman after Your heart. I want to live
> my life in You, through You, for You. I
> acknowledge my sins, my shortcomings,
> and my failure to live up to Your stan-
> dards. Right now I receive Your Son Jesus
> Christ into my needy heart, giving thanks
> that He died on the cross for my sins
> and rose again so I can have eternal life.
> Thank You for giving me Your grace and
> Your strength so I can follow after You!

Talk to God. Give Him your life. You'll be amazed and pleased at the results!

*Lord, I'm so excited to be Your child. I feel Your
incredible love replacing my hurt and my need.
Thank You for being my Savior. Amen.*

The Mary Way

While Martha was so busy trying to get everything in her home in order because Jesus and His disciples were visiting, her sister Mary eagerly sat at her Savior's feet instead of sweeping, cleaning, cooking, and worrying. Are you more like Martha—busy, busy, busy? Or are you willing to set aside time to listen to God like Mary did? Are you reading your Bible and praying regularly? Mary's example is the ideal way to start your morning.

Giving your first thoughts, emotions, concerns, and joys to God is how you can make the choice Mary made. That's how you choose the one thing—time with God—that can never be taken away from you. As you sit at the Lord's feet regularly, you learn to listen to Jesus, linger with Him, delight in Him.

What is your choice today? Tomorrow? Every day?

Lord, sometimes I get too busy with school, chores, friends, and family. I forget to spend time with You. Help me wake up each morning and make the choice to spend time with You. Amen.

An Excellent Trade

Have you ever exchanged a birthday gift? Did you get a crazy sweater two sizes too small and trade it in for a cool one in your favorite color? When you spend time with Christ you get a chance to do something similar... except it isn't about a sweater. You turn over your human abilities, which are too small for the Christian life, and God supplies you with His perfect strength. That's why personal time with God is "the great exchange." When you go to God, you exchange...

> your weakness for His power,
> your darkness for His light,
> your problems for His solutions,
> your frustrations for His peace,
> your hopes for His promises,
> your questions for His answers, and
> the impossible for the possible!

Lord, I have a heart full of things to exchange for Your better version. There is so much I want out of life, and I know true fulfillment and peace and happiness come from You. I'm ready to trade! Amen.

THE HEART OF THE MATTER

God's Word on Love

1. Read 1 Corinthians 13:4-8a. Which part of love is most difficult for you to live out?

2. Because fruit-bearing involves effort on your part, what steps will you take this week toward accomplishing something for God?

3. According to 1 John 4:7-8, who is the source of love?

4. What do verses 20 and 21 of that chapter say about how you can know if someone loves God?

5. What does Romans 5:5 teach about love?

6. And Romans 5:8?

7. Who in your life is hardest to love? As you think about that person, read Jesus' words in Luke 6:27-28. What specific instructions about the person you have in mind does Jesus give you here?

8. What will you do this week to obey each of Jesus' commands? Don't forget to be specific!

Favorite Meeting Place

Aren't all those design shows on TV fascinating? It's amazing how a person's unique style can be brought out in a project. Why not design your own time with God? First consider what hour of the day is best to spend time with God. Next, choose where you'd like to meet Him each day. A comfortable chair in the corner of your room? A bench in the garden? A walk-in closet where you can sit on a throw pillow and enjoy some privacy?

A really fun part of setting up your meeting place is choosing the items and tools that will make your time with God more meaningful. You'll definitely want your Bible, a highlighter, and a journal. You might grab a favorite devotional book...like this one! There are so many clever, colorful notebooks, pens, and Bible covers to choose from. And don't forget praise music. Express yourself. Reflect your taste. Have fun with this!

Your relationship with God is the basis for everything in your life. Make your quiet time personal and exciting!

Lord, I can't wait to express my heart and style as
I spend time with You. When we are talking, I
know You see the unique me You designed. Amen.

List and Listen

A good way to grow in faith in God is to keep a prayer list. Today's a perfect day to start one. Your list may be short at first, but soon your mind and heart will be filled with more physical, emotional, and spiritual needs to bring to God. He's always listening. And as your connection with Jesus grows, you'll be eager to lift up concerns for family, friends, and yourself to Him each day. And when God answers your prayers, you'll be in awe. Remember to take time to listen for His responses during your quiet time and throughout the process of discovering His will.

Have you ever been hungry for prayer? A journal will fuel and feed a deep hunger for this time of talking to God. Get out a notebook and start! This will help you remember what to pray for and inspire you to pray more passionately. When you see and write down how God answers each prayer, your faith will soar!

Lord, I'll start my first prayer list with this prayer for growth in my own faith and prayer life. I can't wait to talk to You and to listen as You answer each of my prayers. Amen.

25

A Weight Lifted

What is your #1 problem today? What makes your heart heavy? Do you worry about your family's well-being? Is a friend struggling? Have you been feeling left out at school? Whatever it is, prayer is the answer. The Bible says to "cast" your problems and burdens on your heavenly Father. Isn't that absolutely great? You get to say to God, "Take all of this stuff from me!" When you do this, you're putting "impossible" problems into His powerful hands. God will take care of them...as only He can.

When you begin each day by giving all the cares of your life to God in prayer, you'll feel the freedom of having a weight lifted from your shoulders and your heart.

Lord, I give You everything that weighs me down. Sometimes I think it is up to me to carry everything that comes my way. But You are offering to take it all on and deal with every problem...even the really hard stuff. Here it is, God. Take it all. Thank You! Amen.

Prayer in Action

Praying and listening to God grows your trust in Him and your knowledge of how He works. What wonderful news! So make prayer a solid habit. How can you put these powerful truths into action in your life?

> Then Jesus told his disciples…they should always pray and not give up (Luke 18:1).

> Cast all your anxiety on him because he cares for you (1 Peter 5:7).

> Where does my help come from? My help comes from the LORD, the Maker of heaven and earth (Psalm 121:1-2).

> Call to me and I will answer (Jeremiah 33:3).

These verses give you a clear look at the blessings that come from praying to God.

Jesus, the desire of my heart is to grow in You. There are so many reasons to put my prayer life into action—to be faithful, to grow, to understand You and life, and to find peace. Help me keep in constant touch with You. Amen.

Spiritual Makeover

If you were given a chance to completely make over your life, would you know what needed to be changed? Can you spot any sin? Any failures in your desire to follow God? Ask God to reveal what needs to be changed. Let Him shed light on your trouble areas through His Word and in answer to your prayers. Maybe you've been gossiping, or telling little lies, or breaking your parents' rules, or making choices that put your purity at risk. Pay attention to what God tells you. It isn't always pleasant, but it is necessary so you can give it to God.

And the good news? Real change takes place as soon as you agree with God (and admit to yourself!) that your behavior, attitudes, or actions are harmful to others or yourself.

Start your spiritual makeover today! What can you turn over to God?

Lord, I have some sins to confess. My time with You has revealed areas that need a makeover. Thank You for making my heart pure again. Amen.

The Prayer Principle

How do you make decisions? If you're like most gals, you make them based on how you feel at the moment of the opportunity. You tend to make physical and emotional decisions instead of spiritual ones. Have you ever skipped out of an opportunity because you were too tired? Have you ever felt like you couldn't handle one more thing so you said no without thinking? Have you ever said yes to something just to avoid further conversation because you were too busy to pray about it?

When life gets crazy or lots of people want you to make decisions, it can be difficult to figure out what is right. Here's a great three-step plan to help you find God's best: 1) Wait to make decisions so that you can... 2) write them down on your prayer list and then... 3) wait on God for direction. Try this out today. You'll stay focused on what God wants you to do, and your time of wondering will shorten or disappear!

God, help me make decisions that are in line with Your will. Guide me so I don't make bad choices because I'm tired, distracted, or pressured. I want to walk through life knowing You are leading me. Amen.

Gettin' the Ingredients Right

Recipes let you gather items from the cupboard, mix them, and get the results you desire. But if you miss an ingredient, what comes out of the oven is going to be a disaster. My daughter Katherine once made brownies for the family...and left out the salt. You know the results! They tasted awful.

Just as a batch of brownies starts with specific food items to become a great dessert to serve with ice cream, several ingredients are key to your becoming a woman who serves God with her whole heart. You can be devoted to God, devoted to His Word, and devoted to prayer...but if obedience is missing from the mix, you will notice the difference. Have you been getting by without obedience? It's time to taste life with the complete recipe for faith.

Lord, obedience is tough for me. I want to argue and go my own way. But I know something is missing from my faith life. Help me add the missing ingredient and serve You with an obedient heart. May the end result be pleasing to You. Amen.

A PERSONAL NOTE FROM

Elizabeth

When I walked into Wal-Mart, my eye was drawn to a large poster picturing several arrogant girls with some pretty awful scowls on their faces. It was an ad for the movie *Mean Girls*.

Now contrast these "mean girls" with my friend Judy who helped me serve at a bridal shower. Judy moved among the women asking if they needed anything and making sure everyone was comfortable. Graciously she refilled cups and removed dirty dishes and soiled napkins. Then I heard one guest sneer as Judy moved out of earshot, "She's too nice."

Since that day I've given much thought to those words: "She's too nice." What Judy did for all of us—including an ungrateful woman—was to actively live out kindness—a fruit of the Spirit. The highest compliment a Christian can receive is to be described as "too nice." When people say that of you and me, we can definitely know we are walking with God and bearing the fruit of His kindness.

In Him,

Elizabeth

On Your Honor

You've probably heard of the Ten Commandments Moses brought down from Mount Sinai. They weren't God's Ten Suggestions—they were commandments. And one of those commandments in Exodus 20:12 states, "Honor your father and your mother, so that you may live long in the land the LORD your God is giving you."

Do you know how to honor your parents? When you listen to them, respect their decisions, and follow their direction, that's a pretty good start. Loving parents are called to teach, train, discipline, and correct their children. Next time you want to fight a rule or argue a point until everybody is upset, remember that honoring your parents is also honoring God.

God, I have to bite my tongue sometimes to avoid dishonoring my parents. When I struggle to show them respect, remind me that they're doing what You ask of them. And I need to do what You want me to do too. Amen.

Home Team Advantage

Have you ever been in a play? Or danced in a ballet? Or been on a sports team? Everyone has to cooperate to make the main event happen, right? It's the same way in a family. God wants families to live together in unity and to glorify Him. Your parents probably aim for this goal too. As part of the team, your job is to cooperate. This involves sacrifice (ouch!). If your parents want you to go to church, you go. If they want to go to church on Wednesday night (and it happens to be the same night as the big event at school), you go to church. If they need you to watch your little brother, you do it. If they need help around the house, you give it.

Cooperation means you have faith in God's best for all His children, including you and your family. This creates the greatest home team advantage.

Lord, I want to be more of a team player at home.
It is painful sometimes! Ease my frustration and
pride with Your peace. Remind me that
cooperation makes us all win in the end. Amen.

Be a Giver

Imagine you are the richest person in the world. Magazines want to interview you. There are a million hits on your website each month because people are fascinated by what you have. People you've never met call daily to ask you to support them. Then imagine yourself walking down a street (or a corridor at school). There you are…throwing your riches away, exuberantly tossing money to everyone you meet. Wouldn't that be amazing?

To experience a rich faith, you need to ask the Lord and your heart, "What can I offer?" in every situation. The answer might be any one of the fruit of the Spirit: love, joy, peace, patience, kindness, goodness, faithfulness, gentleness, and self-control. If you think about it, you have everything to give. You have life in Christ!

God, when I feel like I have nothing to offer others, I know this isn't true. I have the wealth of faith and spiritual blessings from You to share freely. The amazing thing is that I will never run out. I can keep giving and giving from the unending source of Your love. Amen.

An Overflowing Heart

The prayer of Mary, the mother of Jesus, is referred to as "Mary's Magnificat." You can learn a lot about prayer by reading her inspired worship. Mary is expressing her personal joy in the Lord. Here is part of it from Luke 1:46-50:

> My soul glorifies the Lord and my spirit rejoices in God my Savior, for he has been mindful of the humble state of his servant. From now on all generations will call me blessed, for the Mighty One has done great things for me—holy is his name. His mercy extends to those who fear him, from generation to generation.

Let Mary's praises inspire your own. She examines her own life and discovers the ways God has blessed her and others. Her joyful vision of what God has done extends beyond her own circumstances. When was the last time you felt joy? When you need a boost, consider Mary's words and her heart…and do the same.

Jesus, I want to reflect a joy and faith like Mary's. Help me see all You do in my life and for others so I can praise You completely. Amen.

Staying on Course

If you go on a hike tools such as a compass and a map will help you stay on the intended path and reach your destination. Are there tools for staying on God's path? You bet! Pack along the five C's, and you'll be able to stay on the prepared path of God's ways.

Concentrate on doing what is right. Turn to God's Word for direction. **C**ease doing what is wrong. God's strength makes this possible. **C**onfess any sin. Get rid of what holds you back. **C**lear things up with others. Ask for and give forgiveness. **C**ontinue on as soon as possible. Don't get stuck believing you're not worthy of God's love.

In Philippians 3:13-14 God says to forget what is behind so you can spend your energy straining toward what is ahead. If you get off the trail, God will lift you up, dust you off, refresh you, and set you back on His prepared path. The view's much better from here!

God, You're my compass, my guide,
and my path maker. Lead me forward, especially
when I'm scared or off track. I want to follow the
way You prepare for me. Amen.

Brothers and Sisters

I know, sometimes your brothers and sisters get in your way or drive you crazy. But brothers and sisters are a gift! God wants families to love one another and to serve Him. In the Bible there are great examples of brothers and sisters who did wonderful things in faith. Siblings Aaron and Moses and Miriam served God together. Brothers Peter and Andrew followed Jesus and became two of His 12 disciples. Sisters Mary and Martha and their brother, Lazarus, were devoted followers of Jesus and faithfully cared for Him and His disciples.

Look at your family members as people who serve God with you side by side. What changes in your attitude toward your siblings, in your treatment of them, or your expression of love for them could change for the better? The teamwork of ministry and faith is born in the family. And it's born out of love—love for God and love for one another.

Jesus, help me team up with my family to serve You. Show me how my gifts and abilities joined with theirs will do great things if we act out of love for one another and for You. Amen.

Making Friends

Do you wish for more friends? For one great friend? Have you moved or changed schools and face the challenge of making new friends? There's nothing wrong with being a late bloomer in the Friendship Department. Hold out for friendships with those who help you become a better Christian and a better person. And here's a hint—you'll usually find these people at church or in a Christian youth group. It's worth waiting for the right friends.

As a young Christian woman you have so much to give. Treat people the way Jesus wants you to—with kindness, compassion, and love. Everyone needs a smile, a warm hello, and a kind word, especially a word about Jesus. Someone will come along who notices your genuine desire for friendship and will want the same thing. In the meantime, you'll be sharing a great example of Jesus' love with others.

Lord, open my eyes to those around me who need a kind word and encouragement. Help me be strong in my faith so I can connect with others who love You. Thank You for caring about me. Amen.

Getting to the Truth

Have you noticed not everybody has the same beliefs? Even your schoolteachers may have different views and beliefs. Thankfully, as you grow in your faith you'll learn to detect truth and recognize teachings and behaviors that are ungodly. It's like having a built-in spiritual lie detector. If you hear teaching that might conflict with truth, take action:

- Do ask for clarification.
- Do ask for and follow your parents' advice.
- Do ask your pastor, if your parents aren't able to help.
- Do pray about the situation and for wisdom.
- Don't overreact and cause a scene.
- Don't confront the teacher or other students in public.
- Don't show disrespect for authority.

Pay attention to that internal tug of truth. Take your concern to God in prayer. He'll guide you.

God, I don't always know what is right or wrong, but I know You'll help me know what to do. Amen.

THE HEART OF THE MATTER

God's Word on Joy

1. Read 1 Samuel 1:1-18. List some of Hannah's problems.

2. What made the difference in Hannah's attitude, and how was it changed?

3. Read 1 Samuel 1:19–2:1. How did Hannah fulfill her vow?

4. Write out Hannah's sacrifice of praise in 2:1.

5. What was her source of joy?

6. What do you learn about joy from Hannah?

7. Read Acts 16:22-25. List some of Paul's problems.

8. What did Paul do to experience and show his joy in the Lord?

9. List some of your problems. As you think about Hannah and Paul, what can you do right this minute…and this week…to experience the joy of the Lord?

Guy Talk

In your circle of friends, there is probably a boy or two. Or maybe there is a guy in class you'd like to get to know better. You need to be careful when it comes to the opposite sex. Be friendly to everyone, but take a l-o-n-g time when becoming friends with boys. The three things you'll really want to watch out for in your conduct and speech are being *too* friendly, being *too* flattering, and spending *too* much time talking. You don't want to rush into situations that get too serious too fast.

Boys in your youth group can be fun to talk to at barbecues, church events, and family game nights. And boys who are careful in the three areas mentioned above will be the ones who respect your interaction with them. You can still get to know someone without engaging in the flirting that a lot of girls do. Serve God with your behavior, attitudes, purity, and talk.

God, guide me in how much time and energy to spend with boys…and even a special guy. Help me stay true to my desire to know and follow You. Amen.

Let's Be Honest

Let's be honest about honesty. It's not always easy! But being honest paves the way for richer friendships. In Proverbs 27:6 and 9 the Bible says, "Wounds from a friend can be trusted…and the pleasantness of one's friend springs from his earnest counsel." One of the roles of a true friend is to be up front and honest in everything, including correction and advice. You and your true friends should be committed to pulling each other along and pulling each other up toward God's goals for your lives.

And when a friend takes on this role to help you grow in an area where you need help, listen. Don't be too proud or stubborn. Keep an open mind. Thank your friend for caring enough to bring up a difficult subject (you can be sure it wasn't easy!), and then take it to the Lord in prayer. Examine your heart to see if what your friend said is true.

Lord, search my heart and let me know if any
criticism I receive is true. And guide me in what
to do about it. Let me encourage my friends with
honesty too—even when it's hard. Amen.

A Wonderful Witness

When you're around non-Christians be sure to talk about your faith. Bring up everything important to you—Jesus, the Bible, and your church. Sure, they might get put off. They might even decide they want nothing to do with you. Have those possibilities kept you from speaking up? Take heart because the other possibility is beyond great—they might want to know more about the Savior! They might be open to going with you to church or youth group. Maybe they'll even end up in a Bible study with you.

Sharing with non-Christians can be wonderful. Reach out and minister to the people in your life. The best thing you can do for these friends is to find out the details of their lives. Let them know how much you care for them and that you are praying for them. Continually invite them to church or Bible study.

You have the Word of life—the gospel of Jesus Christ. Pass it along!

Jesus, when I'm intimidated to talk about my faith, direct me to say the right things, to be open, and to be myself so others understand how important You are to me and to them…even if they don't know it yet. I love You. Amen.

Lift Them Up

Do you look for the good in your friends…and tell them what you see? Do you give praise and encouragement? The best way to encourage your friends is in the Lord, with Scripture, and through praying together. And when you give a compliment, be specific in your praise. Don't say, "Hey, that was great." Instead say something like, "I always appreciate the way you…" If you catch a friend doing something that's an inspiration to you, tell her. Learn to praise conduct and character. Your goal is to uplift your friend and encourage faith.

Be the first to congratulate a friend who does as well as or better than you on a test. Reach out with a hug when a friend faces a tough day or personal struggle. Be quick to say, "Let's pray!" when you or your friend has needs to lift up to God.

God, I want to encourage, inspire, and lift up my friends. Give me Your heart for the people around me so I see ways to praise them and bring their needs to You. Amen.

The Best Gift to Give

There is no greater gift to give your family and friends than to pray for them—faithfully, regularly, and with your whole heart. Everyone struggles and faces trials and crises. Your friends are dealing with things in their lives they might never share with you. You will never know all the battles being fought in another person's life. But you can pray.

Pray for your friends' spiritual growth, for their schoolwork, for their responsibilities and relationships. Pray for their health, happiness, and commitment to God's purpose. Pray for their problems at home. Spend time in the Bible so you can give your friends specific verses to encourage them. The verse you share might be the perfect insight to get your friend through a tough day.

Focus on the spiritual needs of others. You'll build your Christian walk, and you'll encourage friends to stay true to the path God has for them.

Jesus, give me a huge heart for my friends.
When a friend is in trouble, remind me that I can
do the greatest thing of all—I can talk to You
on his or her behalf. Amen.

Catch the Vision

Have you caught a sneak preview of God's plan for you? It isn't always easy to figure out where God is leading you, but it isn't as complicated as some people think. Isn't that a relief? First, you can relax and know that God calls you to follow the normal flow of events in your life. You are an original creation of His! But there are still the basics of personal faith, school, church, family, and friends to give your days focus. You have your entire life ahead of you, but embrace the part of the plan that's right smack in front of you.

God wants you to excel at what you're doing—homework, sports, sharing your faith, doing chores at home, serving at church. A great benefit of this effort is that you'll earn a good reputation with everyone around you, especially your peers. Even if they don't agree with your faith, your excellence through Christ will be noticed and might open a few doors to share your faith!

Lord, I want to dive into everything I do with
passion. As much as I want to know the future,
I am at peace knowing I'm walking in
Your plan for me. I love growing, learning,
and drawing closer to You. Amen.

Lasting Friendships

You've probably experienced friendships that were short-lived, beginning quickly...and ending just as quickly. So how can you develop friendships that last? Obviously, you need to find the right friends to begin with. But you also need to *be* the right kind of friend. The greatest quality between two friends is loyalty. Have you ever been hurt by a friend's betrayal? It's painful, isn't it? Friends are supposed to be understanding. They don't keep score! If a friend doesn't return a phone call or spends time with someone else, don't get upset. Things happen or come up. Forgive and forget because true friends understand and support each other's commitments and responsibilities. They understand that family comes first, homework is important, and that everyone is super busy. So pray for your friends and be understanding and generous with grace.

Lord, I want to be a great friend to others by showing Your heart and compassion. When my pride or feelings get hurt, remind me to give grace, forgive quickly, and be understanding. Amen.

A PERSONAL NOTE FROM

Elizabeth

My husband, Jim, and I planted 13 ivy vines in our backyard to cover some ugly cement walls. Soon the plants were thriving…except for one. It was absolutely dead! It failed to grow because it had no roots to draw nourishment from the soil. As women after God's own heart we want to grow in Christ. But, just like a plant, we must nurture a healthy, powerful root system deep in the Lord and in His Word, the Bible. We must spend time in prayer and in God's Word.

God's Word creates in us a reservoir of hope and strength in Him. Then, when things get difficult (like when your classmates make fun of your commitment to God…or when you are tempted to give up or give in to something wrong…or when a friend turns on you or gossips about you…or when there is tension at home), you won't be empty. You won't dry up or give up. You can reach down into your hidden reservoir and draw out the strength God provides. Your heart's desire is to flourish…and that requires a strong connection to God!

In Him,

Elizabeth

Stand Up and Stand Out

If someone looked down the packed halls of your school, would your clothes, attitude, and language blend in with the rest of the crowd? If someone followed you around for a few days, would they say you stood out with different beliefs and values from the other kids? If you model Jesus Christ at your school, there will be differences between you and many of the other students. Your days and years spent at school are the training ground for living the Christian life. You must decide who you are living to please—your friends or your friend Jesus?

If you have a hard time living for Christ at school, you'll have a hard time living for Christ later in the work world. This time in your life was created for you to develop a stronger sense of your faith identity. Show your faith. Say it. Live it. Be it. Shout it! Stand up and stand out for Christ today.

God, I so want to live for You! Help me stand out and stand up for You and my beliefs. I want to be different from non-Christians so they can see the strength, hope, and joy I have in You. Help me live You today and every day! Amen.

Reachin' Out

Are you a natural giver? Jesus tells us to give to everyone without expecting to get anything back. Have you ever presented a friend with a wonderful gift, and she didn't thank you in a big way? I'm sure you were disappointed. It's hard not to have expectations when you've done something special. But when you give up expectations and embrace God's way of giving, you stop wondering what the return will be. You become bold with God's heart and understanding. When God puts someone in your path who is suffering or hurting, you won't hesitate to reach out and help. And it won't matter if they thank you or not.

Maybe all the person needs is a shoulder to cry on or someone to pray with her. Maybe the person needs to find someone in authority for assistance. You can help! Reach out and give freely. God will bring people to your path who need encouragement, prayer, and kind words. Be ready to be bold!

God, I have shied away from people in need because I was afraid of what they'd think or I thought I'd get nothing in return. Change my way of thinking so I am open, willing, and excited to share with others without expectations. Amen.

Church Challenge

Are you being a witness at church? Are you wondering, *"What is she talking about? The people at church are already Christians!"* This isn't always the case! Many people are lonely, hurting, and doubting their faith. Maybe they had a big argument with a parent that morning or are facing a really hard week at school. Share your faith and offer your support!

Now for the church challenge! Talk to your girlfriends before church and agree to *not* sit together, walk together, or visit while you're at church. Instead, spread out and connect with others. Introduce yourself to a visitor. Discuss the Sunday school lesson with an older person. Talk to someone you don't normally hang with. You'll discover your church is overflowing with people just like you who want to connect. You and your friends can be the connectors! Divide up—and discover what church is all about.

Lord, give me the courage to step out of my comfort zone so I can grow in faith and compassion. May I take on this challenge to share and inspire my friends to do the same. Amen.

Generous Spirit

There is so much to give that isn't related to your personal possessions (though it's good to give those too). Do you realize you have an endless stash of praise, encouragement, thanks, greetings, kindness, good deeds, and notes of appreciation to offer? You can choose to share these blessings that mean so much to others…or you can be tight-hearted and reluctant to give.

Think about how fabulous you feel when someone lifts you up with a simple comment or bit of praise and support. Why not give that invaluable treasure to others daily? Do you say thank you to your church leaders? Your parents? Your teachers? Even your brothers and sisters? What situations provide great opportunities to encourage a friend or a stranger? Act!

You have amazing wealth, so start giving. Don't hold back!

Lord, I want to give freely. Please grant me a generous heart and spirit. I trust You to provide me with the courage and awareness I need to reach out to others every day. Amen.

Going Pure

Politicians, celebrities, and others are talking a lot about "going green." They want to protect the treasures of the earth. To keep the earth pure or restore it to purity. If you look up the word "pure," you'll discover that it means to be without stain, to be free from pollution, to be clean, to be innocent and guiltless. As important as the earth is, think how truly vital it is to God that you keep yourself free from stains and damage.

God wants you to protect a precious possession—your purity. You probably know how important it is to preserve your physical purity, but did you know your mind is where purity starts? What you think greatly determines how you behave. If you consider yourself unworthy of love, you won't do what it takes to care for your mind, body, and spirit. God wants to be your Protector and Provider. Make keeping your wonderful self pure and righteous for the Lord a priority.

God, when I'm tempted to give up on purity, remind me that I matter greatly to You. Give me the strength and the sense of security I need to protect my heart, mind, and body. Amen.

To the Hilt!

Here are some words that could radically change your life. They are from missionary and Christian martyr Jim Elliot: "Wherever you are, be all there. Live to the hilt every situation you believe to be the will of God." Do you go out into the world each morning expecting God to use you? If not, *why* not? God wants to use you in great ways for His perfect will. He doesn't ask you or expect you to be perfect first!

Before you go anywhere, pray that you will reach out, look out, and be fully available to God's leading. Be in the moment wherever you are. In class take in as much knowledge as you can. During church listen to your pastor's message instead of passing notes or daydreaming. While talking to a friend, focus your heart, mind, and attention on her. God uses a passionate heart to touch the lives of others. When your heart awakens with the desire and longing to serve, give life—and God—your all.

God, as I go out today give me the passion
to be used by You. When I hesitate because
of my insecurities, help me rest in
Your power and purpose and move forward.
I want to live to the hilt! Amen.

The Life of a Hero

Being a superhero comes with a lot of hype (and accessories!)...but that's only in the movies. Being a faith hero requires *internal* attributes. You don't need a cape, but you do need compassion. In the book of 2 Kings, a woman who is referred to as "the Shunammite" in the Bible, saw that the prophet Elisha had no place to stay when he came to town to preach. So she and her husband built a small room on their roof for the prophet and his servant. That's going beyond the call of duty!

This woman looked out and saw a need. She and her husband then reached out and extended a helping hand. They gave out of hearts of love for another person. That is selfless, generous, and heroic. You too can do great things when you begin with goodness. Get ready for action!

Jesus, show me how to be a faith hero.
Let me see where there are needs I can meet.
I want to help! When people cry out, give me ears
to hear and lead me to them. Amen.

Dating God's Way

Dating brings up many questions! At what age should you date? When you date, do you go out as a couple or in a group? Have you and your parents had conversations about this? Do you and your friends talk about it? I'll bet you do! Why not set a high standard? Dare to follow God's very best for you and your boy/girl relationships. Dating can open you up to many temptations. So why not wait until your late teens to date? Before that, concentrate on doing group activities such as youth group gatherings. Honor any dating plans your parents have set for you. Make the choice to remain morally pure…and let your friends know this about you.

When dating becomes a part of your life, be sure you go out with boys who desire to follow God's heart—and that means someone who is an active Christian, a young man whose love for God keeps him committed to God's command for purity in his life…and yours too!

Lord, give me the desire and strength to date with Your standards. I'm going to make keeping pure a priority. Help me honor You, my parents, my body, and my heart. Amen.

THE HEART OF THE MATTER

God's Word on Peace

1. Read Psalm 139. List what you learn about God.

2. List what you learn about God's knowledge of you, your whereabouts, and your situation.

3. List three things you want to remember about God the next time you are in a trying or lonely situation and in need of God's peace.

   •

   •

   •

4. Read Luke 8:22-25 and Mark 4:35-41. Describe the scene. What is going on? Who is present?

5. How did the disciples react to this situation?

6. What was Jesus doing, and how did He respond to the situation? To the disciples?

7. How was Jesus' peace evidenced?

8. List three lessons you want to remember about trusting God in difficult times.

-

-

-

Kick It Up!

On his Food Channel cooking program Chef Emeril's catchphrase "Kick it up!" challenges cooks at home to fix food that knocks the socks off those who eat it. He encourages seasonings and spices to make the flavors explode.

Are you ready to "kick it up" for God? Add the spices of passion and faithfulness to life as you "love the Lord your God with all your heart and with all your soul and with all your mind and with all your strength" just like Jesus said to do in Mark 12:30. When you wholeheartedly embrace His plan for your life, you trade an ordinary life for an incredible, faith-infused life. Don't put your heart on hold. Don't wait for something to happen, to change, to pass, or to improve before you start living a flavorful existence.

Come up with a spiritual catchphrase that encourages you to add zip to your walk with God and promote your commitment to flavorful living.

God, sometimes my faith life doesn't have much flavor. I go through the motions instead of kicking it up! Give me a heart that explodes with amazing, knocks-my-socks-off love for You. Amen.

Where Are You?

Look down. Look around you. Are you on God's path for you? Did you get off course at some point? Sometimes a wrong decision is responsible for a detour. Sometimes God's Word takes second place to other desires and interests…and before you know it your passion for God's plan has waned.

But how's a girl supposed to even know if she gets sidetracked? It isn't like there are traffic signals or signs—the things you rely on when you learn to drive. Look up! Read your Bible each and every day. This act reveals the direction you are headed in, points you in the direction you must go, and helps you make any needed corrections along the way. Commit to the path that leads directly to the heart of God. Your pursuit of His wisdom, His love, and His purpose will keep you on the course He formed for you from the very beginning.

Lord, looking around I see I've stepped away from the path to Your heart in some areas. Remind me through Your Word where I need to be, how to get there, and how much I want Your love and approval. Amen.

Becoming a Dream Girl

When you close your eyes and your head hits the pillow, it's time to dream. You can also dream when you close your eyes and pray. In fact, this dreaming is even more delicious, wonderful, and inspiring because the dreams you have for your life as a person who loves God will become reality. Isn't that incredible! Send up a heartfelt prayer to God, and then let the answers put wings on your dreams.

Tell God about the woman you want to be spiritually in one year. What can you do? Write down your options. Be creative and bold. Describe the leaps and bounds you'd like to make in your faith walk. In one year you can read through the entire Bible. You can be mentored by an older woman. You can mentor a younger sister in Christ. You can attend a Bible study.

Now think about the spiritual woman you'd like to be in 10 years! Start praying…and keep dreaming. God, the shaper of all dreams, is listening.

Jesus, there is so much I want to accomplish, say, become, and experience! My dreams are big because You and Your love for me are so huge and wonderful. I know Your purpose and plan for my life is the path to my dreams. I also know You'll guide me and give me the strength to move forward. Amen.

Devotions "To Go"

Do you take your devotion time out into the world? Do you read this book or another book of devotions in a bunk bed at camp, on your family vacation, in a lounge chair sunbathing around a pool, even in the library after you've finished your homework? Exploring God's Word and His heart for you doesn't have to be an at-home project. It's inspiration, guidance, encouragement, and help to go! The more faithful you are in studying about God during your day, no matter where you are, the more at home you'll be sharing about God throughout your day, wherever you are.

Speaking of sharing, are there any girls at school, or in the neighborhood, or perhaps where you work, you can invite to join in your study? Girls who need the Savior or need to grow in the Lord? Whisper a prayer to God, be bold, and reach out to someone.

God, who can I invite to join me for a study of Your Word? I'm excited about taking my devotional life out into the world! Thank You for the courage and desire to take my faith "to go." Amen.

Big or Small

Big or small...your commitments and decisions matter to God! Don't worry—you aren't troubling Him with your questions. He *wants* you to come to Him. From now on, pray about every opportunity and every decision you face. Should you volunteer at work or school? Accept a date? Go to a party or sleepover? Get a part-time job? Attend college (and which college)? How should you spend your money...or your precious time and energy? Nothing is too small or too big to be prayed over. You are praying to know God's will for every detail of your life...and that's a big thing!

Create a "Decisions to Make" prayer page. Then begin to fill it with the decisions you must make. After all, it's your life. And what you do is important—vitally important!—not only to you, but also to God! List both small and large issues that require your prayers now.

God, I'm amazed that You want to hear all about my life and my decisions. I love that I can come to You with anything...and You listen, You care, and You take me seriously. Thank You. Amen.

Are You Showing Christ?

When you live in Christ, others can see Christ in you. Is this happening in your life now? It can, through God's grace and your decision to being spiritually alive. Be diligent in your habit of reading the Bible. Study it and meditate on it regularly. Make time for prayer. Talking and listening to God is a must for walking with Him. Through prayer you learn more about God, about His heart and purposes. And there is nothing you can't discuss with God! He understands…and nothing surprises Him, regardless of how good or how awful something seems.

Commit to doing what God asks. Make your waking prayer a declaration to love God by making choices that honor Him and His Word. This deep, passionate love leads you to give your heart totally to Jesus. This is when Christ shines through you.

*Jesus, I want to devote my life to You each day.
When I study Your Word and talk to You,
I discover Your heart. I love You, and I want
others to see Your heart through me. Amen.*

A PERSONAL NOTE FROM

Elizabeth

It's truly incredible that you and I can enjoy a relationship with the God of the universe! So now, friend, I am inviting you to make a commitment to prayer. When I decided to learn more about the awesome privilege of prayer, I fully expected all work and no joy. But as I stuck with my desire to develop a meaningful prayer life, I was surprised by the blessings that blossomed in my heart.

I want God's blessings for you too! Remember, desire is half the victory. Write out your dedication to pray. List the people you want to pray for. The next time you pray, read each person's name aloud to God and pray what's on your heart for them.

Begin another prayer list of your own concerns— your #1 problem, some decision you must make, a behavior you'd like to change, a fear that robs you of your peace and joy. Then pray…and experience the many blessings!

In Him,

Elizabeth

Get Enough Fruit

Do you choose fruit during the day? No, not the apple you had for a quick snack after school…but the fruit of the Spirit. These characteristics take shape when you allow God's Spirit to work in you and through you. You can't get them on your own. Relying on God's love will produce love, joy, peace, patience, kindness, goodness, faithfulness, gentleness, and self-control in you. Sounds good, right? So why is it so hard to live these out?

In Galatians 5:17 we learn that "the sinful nature desires what is contrary to the Spirit…They are in conflict with each other, so that you do not do what you want." A part of you will always be at odds with the Spirit. But—praise God!—when you walk or "live by the Spirit," these fruit flourish. Trust God's power and get your nine servings of fruit—spiritual fruit—each day.

Lord, sometimes the stuff I want to do or say gets in the way of following You. Help me resist sin so that the fruit of the Spirit shows in my life. Amen.

Getting It All Together

Have you named Jesus your Savior and Lord? Have you given Him your heart? As the Bible instructs in Romans 10:9, "If you confess with your mouth, 'Jesus is Lord,' and believe in your heart that God raised him from the dead, you will be saved." Before you can experience any spiritual growth, this seed of faith in Jesus must be planted in your heart and life.

So…are you spiritually alive? If you answered no—if you have not accepted Jesus as Lord and Savior—you can set foot on the path of walking with God and growing in Him right now by earnestly praying the prayer below. This is Step 1 toward getting your life together.

Jesus, I know I'm a sinner. I am turning from my sins right now to follow You. I believe You died for my sins and rose again victorious over the power of sin and death. I accept You as my personal Savior. Come into my life, Lord Jesus! Help me obey You and follow You from this day forward. Amen.

Your Special Assignment

You are on a special assignment today. God is asking you to live out His love with anyone and everyone He puts in your path. Does this make you want to back out? Are you hesitant? Or does this responsibility give you the thrill of challenge and the joy of following God's plan?

You can be up to this task if you prepare by gathering and using tools God provides: prayer, the Bible, the fruit of the Spirit, and fellowship, to name a few. Remember, when you are out on assignment, you are never alone. Even on the hard days, when it seems things aren't going smoothly, you have God as your backup. When you need energy, strength, motivation, creativity, and staying power, turn to God. He will fill you again and again with His love for the people you encounter. Everyone God brings into your life is someone He wants to show His love to. Are you ready for your divine assignment?

God, we're in this together, and I love that.
I'm ready to be on special assignment for You.
When I wake up each day, I know You have
called me to love everyone I meet with Your love.
Help me joyfully answer your call. Amen.

Take a Step

Do you crave chocolate more than salad? Of course! It isn't easy to turn your wants toward what is best for you. But you can take control of your body and its cravings when you walk by the Spirit. You do this just like you walk in your physical life—step by step. Live each minute God's way by obeying Him. Seek to please Him with your thoughts, the words you choose to say, and the actions you take.

This doesn't mean you'll wake up tomorrow thinking about carrots instead of a slice of layered chocolate cake dripping with whipped cream frosting. But the more you take on Christ's nature through devotion to Him and His ways, the less your human desires will take over. And God is far more powerful than the allure of cake! Let Him guide you each step of the way!

Jesus, there are many worldly things I long for each day. I give these to You so I can concentrate on the things of faith and truth. Step by step I'll walk in Your Spirit by Your grace. Amen.

63

Share the Love

When someone cuts in front of you at the store, do you hug them? When a friend betrays your trust, do you lift them up to God in prayer? That's not exactly the typical response, is it? As a child of God, you are to love others in the way God and His Son love you. It's hard to love under stressful conditions, yet that's exactly where most of life is lived, isn't it?

When you're tired, hurting, or feeling burdened, you probably want someone to love you and care for you. And you don't feel up to loving other people. But Christian love is an act of the will—a deliberate choice and effort you make. By God's grace you can give love when you want to withhold. You can serve when you want to be served. You can help even when you are hurting. This kind of love comes only from God. He gives it to you to pass on to others.

Lord, thank You for Your grace.
You're an endless source of love I can draw from.
Help me when I'm tired, angry, or hurt.
I want to pass on Your love to others! Amen.

Walk It!

Do you walk the walk not just talk the talk? Do you live out your faith in Jesus? Acting in love is not always easy. When you juggle homework, do your housework, take care of younger siblings, and go to a part-time job, God still calls you to serve and help others. First John 3:18 says we are called to love, not with word or with tongue only, but with actions and in truth. Love has work to do! And love does that work when you take action.

Do you realize every one of your family members gives you an opportunity to put on the work clothes of love? And love has work to do at school as well... and at your job...and at church...and anywhere there are people. So roll up your sleeves and challenge yourself to do the labor of love. Show God's love by your words, attitudes, and actions.

As you look to God for His love, you will get the right attitude—God's attitude—toward sharing and showing love.

God, give me a heart of love for others. Show me
how to put love into action. When I talk about
love lead me to show Your grace in motion. Amen.

Are You Picking Sides?

Do you play favorites with who you give your love to? Don't you find it easy to love "the lovely"—the nice, sweet people who say "thank you!" when you do something for them? The people who appreciate you? Who are kind to you? But what about those who are mean and selfish? Do you love and pray for those who have it out for you? This is what Jesus calls you to do also. That's hard to do!

You're missing out on faith's greatest power if you go through your day picking sides: "These people I'll love; these people aren't nice, they don't deserve love." Do you see it? God expects you to love the hard to love and the unlovely, just as He does. God's love is never deserved—it simply is. I encourage you to stop playing favorites. Ask the Holy Spirit to work in your life so you can love like Jesus.

Lord, keep me from dividing the world into two groups—those I love and those I don't love. When I face the challenge to express love or to pray for someone who has been unkind to me, give me the wonder of Your grace. I can love in Your power! Amen.

The Reward of Love

God's love doesn't involve a payback or reward. Love isn't an exchange. And when you give love to someone in the form of kindness or prayers or a caring chat, you don't wait for something in return. Biblical love is the sacrifice of self.

Self-sacrifice rarely makes the cover of magazines because it often looks weak to the world. But sharing the pure love of God involves your effort, not just your emotion. It demands action. And it is something you *do,* not just something you say.

How are you doing when it comes to loving others? Are you giving up something of yourself? Are you giving to others without expecting the same in return?

Pray for a new heart for others. When you do, you exchange your love for God's love—and no reward can compete with that!

Lord, I've often waited for some kind
of payback for my friendship, good deeds,
and thoughtfulness. But Your love in me asks me
to let go of that expectation. Help me give Your
brand of love to people. Amen.

Sparkle with Joy

One day my daughter Katherine received an unusual phone call. A student at her college had started a business of selling engagement rings. He was making a video catalog of the settings, and he wanted her to model the rings. When she arrived at the studio, the business owner pulled out a piece of black velvet to serve as a backdrop for the diamonds. He explained, "When a diamond is placed against a dark background, the darkness makes it seem more brilliant. And when the diamond is lifted toward light, all of its facets are revealed and allowed to sparkle."

What a perfect picture of joy! True spiritual joy shines brightest against the darkness of trials, tragedy, and testing. And the blacker the background, the greater the brilliance. In the same way, life's dark struggles make Christian joy more dazzling. No matter what you're going through, your joy can sparkle against the backdrop of any situation when you focus on Jesus.

God, I'm facing some hard things in life.
But my hope in You lights up my heart and faith.
I'm learning to trust You in the dark times,
and that makes my joy shine. Amen.

THE HEART OF THE MATTER

God's Word on Patience

1. Read Genesis 6:3-5. What did God observe about mankind (verse 5)?

2. How long did He wait for the inhabitants of the earth to change their ways (verse 3)?

3. Read 1 Peter 2:22-23. Describe Jesus' perfect, sinless conduct (verse 22).

4. Yet how was Jesus treated (verse 23)?

5. How did Jesus exhibit patience toward those who put Him to death?

6. Read 2 Timothy 2:24-26. Write out the different words and phrases that indicate patience (verse 25).

7. What might be the outcome of such patience according to verses 25-26?

8. Read 1 Thessalonians 5:14. What bottom-line principle for patience is stated here?

9. As you review the teaching from these scriptures regarding patience, list three things you want to remember—or remember to do—to better handle any people problems.

-

-

-

Better Than Happiness

Your parents and friends want to see you happy. God wants to see you joyful. What's the difference? Joy comes from the Lord. And it can be experienced anywhere at anytime. It isn't related to or dependent on your situation. Because you take your relationship with Jesus everywhere you go, you can experience joy in Him no matter what's happening to you.

Before His crucifixion, Jesus described the special relationship He will have with His disciples if they abide in His love. In John 15:11 He says, "I have told you this so that my joy may be in you and that your joy may be complete." He wanted His disciples to know the joy of fellowship with Him. This is how much Jesus loves you too! He wants you to know the amazing joy and gift of togetherness with Him. Dedicate your life to Him and experience this tremendous sense of belonging and joy!

Jesus, my happiness comes and goes with the day... sometimes even by the hour. I want Your joy that fills me all the time. You care about me so much. Thank You. I'm so glad I'm Your child! Amen.

Has the Seed Been Planted?

If you aren't sure if the seed of faith has taken root in your heart, you may want to say a prayer of recommitment. You could pray:

Jesus, I know that in the past I asked You into my life. I thought at that time I was Your child, but my life hasn't shown the fruit of my belief. I want to make a real commitment to You, making You the Lord and Master of my life. Amen.

If you're not sure where you stand with God, let Him know right now in prayer. Don't worry about the words. Just share your heart. God loves you and knows your desire. He wants to be close to you.

If you can say, "Yes! I know I'm alive in Christ now and forever!" take a few moments to thank God and praise Him for all that Jesus did for you. Make a fresh pledge to walk with Him in obedience for greater spiritual growth.

Jesus, I commit all areas of my life to You. I give You my today and my tomorrows. I praise You for who You are...my Savior, my Lord, my Friend, and the Creator of everything I am and will become. Amen.

Forever Joy

What's your mood like right this minute? What was it an hour ago? Your mood and your sense of happiness are always changing. But your spiritual joy is rooted in your unchanging God. That's right. Your joy is permanent. In John 16:22 Jesus says that "no one will take away your joy." However, one thing that can rob you of the joy God provides is failing to walk with Him. But when you live by the Holy Spirit, He produces joy in your life as you walk in obedience to His ways.

There is something incredible about joy—it is always available. Joy is rooted in your ever-present God, and it's not going anywhere. Whatever your circumstances, you have access to the source of true joy anytime you turn to God. Yes, life can get you down. Certainly there are people in your life who can do the same. Do you face days when you are just getting by? Turn to God and receive your endless portion of deep, never-changing, always available, transforming joy.

Jesus, I seek Your joy today. Fill me up.
No one can take away my joy in You.
No situation can limit the joy You give. I know You
are here for me and Your joy is deeper than
the greatest trial I will ever face. Amen.

The Sacrifice of Praise

Cultivate joy in your life by thinking of joy as the sacrifice of praise. Let me explain. When life is good, praise and thanksgiving flow freely from your heart and lips. But when life turns dark, praise and thanksgiving don't flow quite so easily, do they? Instead, you have to choose to follow God's advice in 1 Thessalonians 5:18 to "give thanks in all circumstances, for this is God's will for you in Christ Jesus." When you don't feel like praising the Lord or thanking Him, and yet you do what God says, that effort makes your praise "a sacrifice."

At those times when you'd rather indulge in self-pity or stay stuck in depression, choosing to look beyond your pain makes your praise to God a sacrifice. Choosing to praise God in all circumstances is a remarkable adventure in faith. When you act out of obedience, God will fill the void of sacrifice with His amazing joy and love.

Lord, I give You praise! Give me the
strength to offer up thanksgiving even when
I don't feel like it. I know You are worthy of
praise each and every day. Amen.

A Dose of Joy

What lifts your spirits? Is it a call or email from a friend? A good grade on a test? Praise from your parents? Do you turn to God for that lift when you need it? There are many reasons to turn to God for a boost that endures. You can experience the wonder of God's promises every day. So give yourself the gift of joy. Write out some of God's promises from the Bible on separate slips of paper. Every morning pick a promise to read and keep with you during the day. Think on that promise often and see how God is true to His Word. Make this a fun project for the whole family. At dinner you can share with each other how God kept His promises all day.

If you are struggling with something right now, turn to the treasure of God's precious promises. Find joy in them. Do you need a dose of joy? All you have to do is focus on God.

God, Thank You for Your promises...and for keeping them! When I look at them, I realize Your love is so great. Give me a dose of Your joy today, Lord. It changes me from the inside out and gives me great hope. Amen.

No More Fear

The late newspaper columnist Ann Landers was once asked if any one problem stood out in the more than 10,000 letters she received in the mail each week. Her answer? Fear. Causes for fear surround us on every side. But here's good news for you as a Christian! You have a built-in resource for handling fears. That's right! You have the peace of God. It is different from any remedy you could ever find anywhere!

Life is like a roller coaster, but you can experience God's peace no matter what is happening. How? Walking by His Spirit. You are blessed with what Philippians 4:7 calls "the peace of God, which transcends all understanding." It's right there in the very middle of your trials…when you look to God.

Jesus, sometimes life feels like it is spinning out of control. I look to You for Your peace. I can't calm the world, but I can seek Your healing, Your peace, and the safety of Your arms. Amen.

With Every Step

Here's a fact of life: Until we are with the Lord, there will always be suffering. So...what trial is causing you the greatest grief, the sharpest pain, the deepest sorrow today? Is it a disappointment, a dashed dream, a disaster, a disability? Is it loneliness? Difficulty with your family? An unknown future as you look down the road of life?

Whatever your greatest trial is today, let it cause you to turn to God. Offer Him a sacrifice of praise and allow yourself to be touched by Him, the only source of true joy. Your heart can be filled with genuine joy— spiritual joy—when you walk with God through your trials, praising Him with every step and breath. That's an attitude of joy! Develop it. Cultivate it. Live it.

Jesus, I will praise you with every step and breath
I take today. You've changed my heart and mind.
I give You my praise, my worship, my time,
my heart, and my life. Amen.

A PERSONAL NOTE FROM

Elizabeth

The first thing I see every morning when I open my front door are my flowers. One look at them slumping over tells me they need water! So every day I get out my watering bucket, go to the faucet, fill up the bucket, and carry water to these poor little plants. I know that if I don't fill my bucket and give my flowers life-giving water, they will die. Even when I don't feel like watering them, I do it anyway. I act on my will, not my feelings. I put forth the effort to keep the flowers alive.

Why don't you view the challenge of loving all the people God puts in your path in the same way I view caring for my flowers? You might not feel like loving them, but God wants you to. Allow Him to fill you with His life-giving love so you can pour out His love into the lives of thirsty, needy people. They will be blessed…and so will you.

In His amazing love,

Elizabeth

Hold Back

Which is easier—to give in to emotions and anger when someone hurts you or practice patience and hold back your wrath? To lash out with cruel words or hold back your hateful words? It's easy to let go, lose your temper, and tell the offender exactly how you feel and what you think! But much harder is the godly response—God's response!—of choosing to do nothing outwardly as you resist in patience inwardly.

Ask God for the strength and grace to do nothing when you want to react negatively! When you resist in patience, you practice endurance. This is for the good of others and for yourself. As you interact with people each day, pain sometimes comes. But God's Spirit can help you do nothing as you pray and seek wisdom. After asking for patience, it's time to make a move, to go into action, to get up and do something good. Follow God's will!

God, only Your strength can keep my temper under control. I've tried to do it on my own, and that didn't turn out so great. Please give me patience. I don't like it when I feel out of control. I'd rather live in Your will! Amen.

It's a Joy Thing!

True spiritual joy is not happiness. "Happiness" is an emotion, a state of good fortune and success related to your circumstances. If all is going well, you are happy, but as soon as some dark cloud or irritation enters your life, feelings of happiness vanish.

In the middle of pain and sorrow, God's joy is a grace gift. He gives His joy to you as you encounter the hardships, problems, and persecutions of life. This supernatural joy, given through God's Spirit, is more powerful than all the tough conditions of life. As God's child, you can experience and enjoy God's joy regardless of what life entails. That's because your joy as a Christian is not dependent on your efforts, emotions, accomplishments, or circumstances. Instead your joy is based on the spiritual realities of God's goodness, His complete love for you, and His ultimate victory over sin and darkness. God's joy is always here for you.

Lord, in the middle of my hard times You are my source of joy. I am thankful that this peace and joy does not depend on my abilities or success, but comes from You and Your never-ending grace. Amen.

God of Promise

What is on your "Great List of Things to Worry About"? Worrying about what others think of you? Worrying about what you look like—if you're too fat or too thin, if you're pretty enough? Worrying about health, safety, boyfriends, dating, the future? About getting up in front of others or an upcoming social event? About your brother or sister or parents?

Over 300 times in the New Testament God commands us to not be anxious. Philippians 4:6-7 says, "Do not be anxious about anything, but in everything by prayer and petition, with thanksgiving, present your requests to God. And the peace of God, which transcends all understanding, will guard your hearts and minds in Christ Jesus."

Write this verse on a card and say it to yourself often. Carry God's command with you—physically on the card and spiritually in your heart. God's active and powerful Word will begin to change your heart and mind. You'll go from worrying to worshiping as you trust the God of the promise.

God, I will keep Your Word close to my heart. I want to meditate on Your truths so that I don't give in to worry. Thank You for Your promises. Amen.

Choosing Peace

Are you quick to hit the panic button? I have great news for you! When you feel like a nervous wreck you have a choice. Give in to those feelings or be filled with God's peace. Here's how it works You experience God's peace…

- when you *choose* not to panic…but to rest in God's presence,
- when you *release* your terror…and trust in God's wisdom and ways,
- when you *reject* your nervousness…and remember God is in control,
- when you *ignore* your dread…and instead accept God's dealings.

Just think…you can take your next test full of peace instead of panic. Try out for a part in a play or audition for the choir with complete trust in God for the outcome. Yes, God expects you to do the preparation work. But He will be with you from the beginning to the end!

Lord, fill me with Your peace. Help me rest in You when I'm tempted to panic or worry. Amen.

Faith's First Response

When you're in trouble, you've got a built-in first response. Prayer. And by "trouble" I don't mean just when you've done something wrong, but also when you have a problem and desperately need God's intervention. Go to God for help with your needs. Sure, you might have a long list! That's okay. School problems, people problems, parent problems, friend problems, boyfriend problems, loneliness problems. Add to this list your doubts and worries, and it's easy to see your tremendous need for prayer!

In Ephesians 6:18 Christians are instructed to "pray in the Spirit on all occasions with all kinds of prayers and requests." In other words, there is something you can—and should!—do about the pressing needs in your life. You are to pray to God—to talk over your specific concerns with Him, with the God of the universe.

God, I've got a lot to unload today. You asked me to come to You...so here I am. My requests are big and small. My need for You is great. And my dependence on You is growing each day. Thank You for being here for me 24/7. Amen.

Following God's Way

How are you at following God's directions for your life? When something tough comes along that requires more than you want to give, do you say, "Oh, thanks, but I won't be able to do that." Or maybe you struggle through everything by your own power, alone and stubborn, never asking the Father for His strength. Each time you do this, you're deciding to live without love, joy, and peace.

You're missing out! Turn to the Father, resist the desire to go it alone, and rest in His presence until you realize His fruit of love, joy, and peace. Spend however long it takes in prayer, study, and meditation to allow Him to fill you with Himself until He has all of you.

Jesus, forgive me for doing everything on my own.
I want to stop going it alone. I want to turn to
You for strength so I depend on and experience
Your amazing love, joy, and peace. Amen.

Changing the World

Today commit yourself to God completely and change the world for Christ. Rush to Him in prayer and remember His promises when you need love, when you need joy, and when you need peace. Stay there until you have them. If you will commit yourself to spending time with the Father, the effects are limitless! Commitment to diligent prayer means allowing Christ in to change your heart, your relationships, your family, your friends, your school, your neighborhood, and your world. And He will do it! Without Him, you only go through the motions, giving little to family, friends, strangers, and a world that needs so much.

Are you ready to change the world? Did you ever think that was possible? With God working through you, you'll take on the transforming, life-changing and—Yes!—world-changing attitudes of love, joy, and peace.

God, change me. Give me the desire to be with You in prayer daily. Help me keep my commitment to You. I want to help You change the world. I want Your attitudes of love, joy, and peace. Amen.

Keep Your Connection!

Don't you love having access to wireless internet service! You can get information anytime you need it. You can communicate with most anyone from anywhere. When you spend devotion time with God, you're taking advantage of your complete access to the Creator. And you're keeping your connection to God strong. Here's how it works. If you start each morning with your Bible reading, a time of study, and prayer, you're saying to God, "I'm in this to know you better!"

As you continue with your day, you'll experience a stronger sense of God's presence. You've already interacted with Him, so talking with Him and following His will is much easier. Distractions come up all day long. Good ones. Bad ones. And all-consuming ones. A friend is in a sour mood. You feel rejected. A test doesn't go well. You miss your ride home from school. These could be points of disconnection between you and God. But a heart tied to the Lord's from the beginning of the day keeps its signal strong.

Lord, when I communicate with You, I feel closer to Your heart. I seek Your guidance and give You praise more easily throughout the day. Thank You for the strong heart-to-heart connection we have. Amen.

THE HEART OF THE MATTER

God's Word on Kindness

1. Read 2 Samuel 9:1-7. What question did David ask when he became king of Israel (verse 1)?

2. What did he do or what actions of kindness did he take when his question was answered (verses 2-7)?

3. Read 2 Kings 4:8-10. How did the Shunammite woman show kindness? And to whom?

4. Read Acts 9:36. Describe Dorcas' many acts of kindness.

5. What did she do for the widows in her community (verse 39)?

6. Read Luke 9:12-13. For whom was Jesus concerned?

7. How did Jesus' actions and concerns differ from the disciples' behavior?

8. What do these four examples (David, the Shunammite woman, Dorcas, Jesus) reveal about how you show—or don't show—kindness? And what do you plan to do about growing in kindness?

Adorn Your Heart

Are you completely dressed? Well, of course, you've dressed your body with clothes, but did you know you're supposed to dress your spirit with the godly quality of patience? In Colossians 3:12, the Bible instructs you to clothe yourself with patience. How do you do this? By being patient when you see faults in other people or are annoyed by them in any way…instead of being irritated or critical or lashing out.

Who irritates you the most and why? When you dress in patience, you'll listen longer and more carefully. You'll strive to help others without making a big deal of it. And you'll wait for situations to improve, rather than dwell on difficulties. Did you ever think that with one piece of "clothing" you could change your life and relationships for the better? Adorn yourself with a heart of patience and wear it with style!

God, my days often turn for the worse when I get impatient with friends or my parents. Please give me patience so I show others a loving attitude and a willingness to wait for Your leading. Amen.

How Doing Nothing Changes You

Have you ever been told to do nothing? That might seem a bit strange, if not a bit lazy! But when this advice is given in the context of patience, it's an excellent suggestion. Patience is love doing nothing. Take a look at a recent situation when you were irritated, aggravated, or frustrated. How did that go for you? When your emotions are on edge, chances are your responses are based on anger. Think ahead to situations that might make you feel that way. What if you hold back your smart-mouth response or your scowl? What if you stay put rather than walk away in anger?

Doing nothing gives you time (even if only seconds!) to quietly do something—to pray, to reflect, to ask for advice, and to plan to respond in a good, better, or best way. First go to God for His patience…and then do as He would do! (And just a hint—this process is usually helped along by praying.)

God, remind me to come to You in prayer before I say or do anything out of anger. Please turn my negative situations into opportunities to serve You and to show Your patient nature and love to others. Amen.

Flexing Your Patience Muscles

Proverbs 19:11 says, "A man's wisdom gives him patience; it is to his glory to overlook an offense." With God's power and strength you can hold back your anger. There are ways to develop your muscles of patience, to lengthen your fuse.

- Pray and ask God to give you His patience.
- Avoid conflicts as much as possible.
- Be careful in your responses to others and your actions.
- Follow Jesus' example.

The Bible says in 1 Peter 2:22-23 that Jesus "committed no sin, and no deceit was found in his mouth. When they hurled their insults at him, he did not retaliate; when he suffered, he made no threats." Ask God to help you respond like Jesus. When you're injured by others or flat out annoyed by them, turn your bad temper and your hurt heavenward. With God's help you'll have the power of patience.

Jesus, lead me away from my first response when people are slow, unfair, unjust, or unkind. Help me develop my patience muscles. Amen.

Now for Some Action

Kindness is a fruit of the Spirit that calls you to action! It actively asks, "Who needs love? How can I ease someone's burden? How can I touch another person?"

Often you can share this fruit of the Spirit with simple gestures, small actions, and uplifting words that encourage someone in a moment of need, hurt, crisis, or just because. Do you consider the feelings and concerns of your friends? Your parents? Your teachers? Then follow through with reassuring comments and generous, sincere offers of help. If you see a fellow student who is tired or sad or poor, do you judge her or does your heart open up with compassion and a desire to help?

Kindness encourages action that builds up others and seeks ways to be of service and comfort.

Lord, reveal to me the needs of others.
I'm so busy with my life and my concerns that
I miss out on the chance to act out of a heart
of kindness. Show me how to extend Your grace
to people in ways that lift them up. Amen.

Covering Your Life

Do you pray about the big things, but forget to pray for your daily needs? Relying on God for everything is a gift of faith. Pray for energy and endurance, for focus and staying power so you can continue moving toward the goal of getting your work done, whether that's homework, housework, or at a job. If you have a job babysitting or working part-time somewhere, your prayers should include your workplace, your workmates, and your faithfulness on the job. Pray to work willingly and eagerly with your heart and hands.

And don't leave out your relationships with parents and family members. Pray over them too. There are also friendships and a desire for companionship (both male and female) that can be talked over with God. Pray, as Romans 12:18 says, to "live at peace with everyone." Give your life to the Lord by covering it in prayer— every second of it.

God, please fill me with the energy I need to honor You with the work I do. And give me a heart that is quick to pray for the people around me. May my actions and relationships honor You always. Amen.

Watching for a Changed Heart

A sure sign that God is answering your prayers for greater compassion is when you find yourself looking at people and thinking, *What would help her? What would help him? What does he need? What does she need?* When you ask God, *How can I serve this person? How can I make his or her life easier? How can I touch her life and lift her burden?*

Kindness takes action, and that requires thought and prayer. Can you think of someone you can be kind to? Now make plans to express your care. Ask God to give you a loving heart and a creative mind. Look around for the needs of people in your home, your neighborhood, your workplace, and your church. Hurting people are literally everywhere! What can you do today to touch another life with kindness?

Lord, who can I reach today with extra attention, support, or a vote of confidence? Help me be creative with my efforts of kindness to meet the needs of people on a personal, spiritual level. Amen.

Open Eyes, Open Heart

You can care for people in the same way God cares for you…just by paying attention and being on the lookout for people's needs. In fact, 1 Peter 3:12 says that this is one of the ways God cares for us: "The eyes of the Lord are on the righteous and his ears are attentive to their prayer." You can love as God loves.

Look to God for His help with any unkind emotions and thoughts you have about others. Then obey God's commands for kindness. Constantly ask God to work in your heart to help you care, think, and notice the people He places in your life. Use your God-given capacity for observation. As Proverbs 20:12 says, "Ears that hear and eyes that see—the Lord has made them both." As you go about your day, keep this simple reminder in your thoughts: Observe and serve!

Jesus, give me wide eyes and open ears.
Keep me from passing judgment on others.
When I get stuck on first impressions, teach me
to truly see the hearts of people. Amen.

A PERSONAL NOTE FROM

Elizabeth

Why are we rarely satisfied? Why do we think everyone else has what we want? Think a minute about the things you worry about. Now let's look at one of God's guidelines for contentment in Philippians 4:6-7, "Do not be anxious about anything, but in everything, by prayer and petition, with thanksgiving, present your requests to God. And the peace of God, which transcends all understanding, will guard your hearts and your minds in Christ Jesus." And here's another great one in verses 11 through 13, "I have learned to be content whatever the circumstances....I have learned the secret of being content in any and every situation....I can do everything through him who gives me strength."

Thank the Lord that contentment is yours when you pray! Look at your list of wants and worries. How will you put today's scriptures to work the next time you worry? God doesn't want you to waste your energy on worry. Instead, turn to Him!

In Him,

Elizabeth

Faith Starts at Home

Do you save your good behavior for church? Do you treat your friends with loyalty, generosity, and thoughtfulness...and treat your parents and siblings with a little less love? While it is important to be a strong Christian witness to those outside your household, keep in mind this truth: What you are at home reflects what you are. It's at home where you relax and "be yourself," which reveals your true character and faith.

Live out God's command to be kind to others at home. Pray every day this week for God to fill your heart with His compassion. Then write out how praying for compassion made a difference in you, your week, and your family. Think of ways to help your parents and your brothers, sisters, and even your grandparents. Make it your goal to make their lives easier. What can—and will—you do today?

God, help me be kind and thoughtful to my family. When I start treating them with less compassion, give me a new heart, a new perspective. I want to serve them with love and respect and honor You in my home. Amen.

How Does Your Garden Grow?

Just as a garden is laid out by a plan, God designs your life according to a plan. He uses the people, events, and circumstances in your life to guide you along the path toward godliness. Truly, He knows how to grow you to be like Him!

Three fruit of the Spirit that help your life's garden plan thrive are patience, kindness, and goodness. Patience is like a seed hidden in the earth, out of view, while it secretly and slowly nurtures life. Kindness grows from the seed of patience in the dark depths where it develops a root system. It pushes its head up through the soil until, at last, it cracks through the soil, visible to all. Goodness blossoms and blesses all who see it.

Do others see patience, kindness, and goodness being planted, taking root, and blooming in you? Spend time in God's Word to give these fruit of the Spirit food and light and protection so you can see the harvest in your life.

God, am I cultivating patience, kindness, and goodness? Help me seek Your direction and love so I can follow the design You have for my life. Amen.

Getting a Handle on Goodness

Thank goodness for God! Or better still, thank God for goodness. From cover to cover the Bible tells the story of God's goodness and how He gives it to His people. But this goodness in you isn't about being perfect or "acting" nice when you really want to scream. Godly goodness is a spiritual grace that develops as you grow in faith and obedience.

While kindness plans to do something good for others, goodness is all about action. God in you and His presence with you produces His goodness in you. This goodness, in turn, seeks to serve others. It's dedicated to helping others. Your family and friends, your church and school—the whole world!—need people who are actively kind. The world needs people who walk out their doors every day ready to do good—not just think about it or pray about it, but really do it. Are you ready to be that kind of person—for goodness' sake?

Jesus, when my goodness fails, I realize
I need Your grace and goodness. Fill me with it
every day so I become actively kind and a
strong witness for You. Amen.

Choosing to Be Like Christ

Susan was hurt by non-Christians at school who openly despised her for being one. "No matter what others at school do or say to me, I have decided I'm going to respond in goodness and be a good advertisement for Christ. And it's already working!"

Ann too was hurt—but by the Christians in her church youth group. "I chose to not feel hurt when I was not invited to join them in their activities. I chose to not feel bitterness or resentment. I chose to show my love for them."

Maria faced a hostile boss at her part-time job. She decided to respond God's way. "I had to make a choice—give back what he is dishing out or show him the kindness and goodness of the Lord."

Like these young women, your walk with God requires many decisions on your part as you constantly look to God and ask Him, "What is the right thing to do?"

Lord, help me choose Your way. When I encounter hurtful people or comments, I want to counter them with Christ-like behavior. Amen.

Does Your Heart Show?

A heart of faithfulness shows in your words and your actions, your behavior and your attitude. When you're walking with God by His Spirit, you and others will notice:

- You follow through...on what you have to do.
- You come through...no matter what.
- You deliver the goods...whether a returned item or a school paper.
- You show up...early so others won't worry.
- You keep your word and commitments.
- You go to church regularly...and don't neglect worship.
- You're devoted to duty...just as Jesus was when He came to do His Father's will.

Which of these are evident in your life? Which do you need to work on? Ask for God's strength and for a heart of faithfulness that shows in every part of your life.

Lord, where is my heart of faithfulness showing? Where is it not? I will lean on Your strength today so I can speak and act with grace and faithfulness. Amen.

The Land of Opposites

Sometimes you need to see the opposite of what's good and what works to get the point. For instance, one of the opposites of faithful is fickle. You've met people who change their minds, change their loyalties, change their standards. Nothing seems to matter or be that important. Nothing seems worth authentic commitment.

Another opposite of faithful is unreliable. An unreliable person doesn't come through, can't be depended on, and can't be trusted with information or responsibility.

Have you struggled to get along with someone with these behaviors? It's almost impossible to maintain a relationship when one person is not faithful and dependable. How can you be a more faithful friend and follower of Christ?

As the saying goes, you may depend on the Lord—but may He depend on you? When you start leaning toward what not to do, return your focus to God.

God, I want to walk in Your footsteps and be consistent in my decisions, actions, and faith. Let me be a good friend to others and a loving daughter to You, my heavenly Father. Amen.

Faith Work

How are you at doing your homework? Fast and fastidious? Slow and sloppy? Do you realize your homework is not just an assignment from your teacher, but it's actually from God? It's true! Whatever you are doing, you are called to do it well. Homework is just one of the many assignments from God, and there's no way to accomplish them without faithfulness. You show your faithfulness when you follow through with your daily devotions, prayer, and Bible reading. God sees your loyal heart when you are faithful to your friends and stand with them as you face the challenges of school. Your heart shows when you share Jesus with those who don't know Him. And where you are on church day reflects your faithfulness. Attend church regularly to fuel your spiritual growth, to serve God's people, and to worship faithfully.

You affect the world and the future by committing to the personal assignments God is giving you today. Now, what about that homework?

Lord, when I get lazy with my devotions,
my homework, my efforts to help at home, help
me remember that these are part of
Your plan for me. Amen.

Struggling to Be Faithful

Even a woman of promise struggles with excuses. Do any of these sound familiar? Tiredness moans, "I can't get up...I can't make it to church...I'm just too tired!" Laziness whines, "I don't want to do my work chores, I'd rather hang out." Hopelessness asks, "Why try?" and then gives up. Procrastination kills faithfulness and announces, "I'll prepare for that class later... I'll read my Bible later." Rationalization says, "Someone else will do it." Apathy shrugs, "I don't care if the dishes get done...I don't care if I'm faithful." Rebellion says, "I won't do what the Bible says...I won't do what my parents ask...I won't follow through."

Praise God that you can go to Him when you are feeling tired, lazy, uncommitted, sick, and sorry for yourself. You can find in Him the strength (His strength), the vision (His vision), and the faithfulness (His faithfulness) to counter these attitudes. When you lose the lies and excuses, you'll discover God's truth and excellence!

God, deliver me from my excuses. I want to hold on to Your promises and truth. Amen.

THE HEART OF THE MATTER

God's Word on Goodness

1. What do these verses say about doing good?

   Luke 6:27-28—

   Romans 2:7—

   Romans 2:10—

   Romans 12:21—

   Galatians 6:10—

2. Which of those verses are your favorites? Why?
   (You may want to write them down in the back
   of this book.)

3. Which of those verses are the most challenging?
   Why?

4. What actions did the following women take that modeled goodness—the desire to do something?

Rebekah (Genesis 24:15-20)—

The Shunammite woman (2 Kings 4:8-10)—

Martha and Mary (Luke 10:38 and John 12:2)—

Dorcas (Acts 9:36)—

Lydia (Acts 16:15)—

5. Which of these women and their acts of goodness inspires you most to minister goodness to others, and why?

Growing Gentleness

In Matthew 5:5 Jesus says, "Blessed are the meek, for they will inherit the earth." Have you ever been meek on purpose? That sounds so wimpy, so wishy-washy, so undesirable, doesn't it? But look at meekness from God's view: Meekness is gentleness. And gentleness is not resentful, it bears no grudge, and it is not involved in rehashing present or past injuries. What do you do instead when facing a challenge? You find refuge in the Lord. You trust the Lord for every fruit of the Spirit—and gentleness is one of them.

But how can you take someone calling you names or spreading gossip about you or causing you pain? The answer boils down to your faith. Faith believes He will help you handle everything that happens in your life in a positive way—His way. Your faith in God keeps you from struggling and fighting because faith believes God can and will help you! It believes God will fight for you when necessary!

Jesus, when I face conflict or someone towering over me with power, I can be meek and gentle and unafraid because You are here to fight for me. Thank You. Amen.

Admission to Submission

When you want to see a play or a movie, you first buy a ticket. And then you give that ticket to someone who directs you to the right theater. You probably don't think much about handing over that ticket because your goal is to see a great show. When you want to see and experience your new life in Christ, you hand over your current life—every part of it—to God so that He can direct You to the right path. The right purpose. And the righteous life.

You may not be sure you like what "submission" implies. But maybe you're too focused on your "ticket" instead of on where you're going. Following God in every way for every thing isn't about giving up, it's about giving yourself to the Master and Savior. And that leads to something much bigger than a box-office hit!

Jesus, here's my ticket…my life. Take it from me and direct me toward the purpose You have planned for me! I'm excited to follow Your lead. I want to hand over my life to You—100 percent! Amen.

Where's Your Strength?

Do you ride your bike, do a lot of yard work, or play sports? If so, you probably have muscles to show for it. When you're walking by the Spirit and exercising your spiritual strength in the Lord, God's self-control will show in your life! Here's what it looks like:

- Self-control controls and checks the self.
- Self-control restrains the self.
- Self-control disciplines and masters the self.
- Self-control says "No!" to self.

Here's what one woman did to gain victory over a problem. She wrote this list on a 3" x 5" card and taped it on the bathroom mirror to help her with her problem of overeating. What a great idea! And you know what? Because the list applies to all problems, why not make one for yourself? These steps will remind you often of God's pattern for self-control.

Lord, I have victory over temptation, sin, and difficulties because of Your strength. I want to walk in the Spirit so there is evidence of self-control in my life. Help me be obedient to Your will. Amen.

Refuse to Be Anything Less

Does your life show the fruit of gentleness? Do you submit to God and His management of your life? Do you consider God's meekness a strength? Do you release grudges? Are you able to look beyond the hurts caused by someone else…right to the God of wisdom?

When you believe and trust that God knows what He is doing in your life, you'll find the strong, solid, amazing peace required for being gentle. Invest in your prayer life and you'll reap the reward of gentle habits—bowing, bending, kneeling, yielding, and submitting in spirit to God. When you leave your time of prayer and step into your day, you can say no to complaining and grumbling, and say yes to nothing less than 100-percent gentleness.

Lord, forgive me for holding a grudge.
I've carried it with me instead of giving it and
the situation over to Your strength. May I turn to
Your wisdom and say yes to gentleness. Amen.

The Freedom of Control

When every fiber of your being wants to be angry and blow up, does anything hold you back? You probably aren't thinking about love, joy, and peace when sarcasm rises up or you want to slam a door! But godly self-control helps you choose each of those—even when you're moody, even when you're tempted to get boiling mad.

How great that you can rest in the Spirit's self-control. Only God can give you the strength and gentleness to "take it." To ignore the negative comments. To resist payback when a sibling throws away your homework page. "Taking it" requires some serious power. The fruit of self-control given by the Holy Spirit is that serious power. And it's a rock-solid foundation for your journey to be like Jesus!

Jesus, you've seen me when I get mad and it isn't pretty! I always regret it. Help me to live without that regret by holding my tongue and accessing Your control. Amen.

Resistance Exercises

What is your biggest temptation? Maybe you have more than one that gets you stuck in bad habits. Is your stumbling block chocolate cake, gossip, materialism, dwelling on negative comments, impure thoughts? Maybe your struggle isn't that big right now. But over time each area of temptation can turn into more: More comfort eating. More talking about people. More spending. More fear and insecurity. More impure desires.

What would the blessings of not giving in to the flesh be? Exercising resistance will give you God's victory in this situation. Plus, by saying no to small temptations, you build a track record with God and gain experience that will help you later when you face a larger temptation.

Lord, help me experience the blessing of resisting temptation. Give me the power to say no to temptations. I want to be victorious in Your strength in the big and small areas. Amen.

Power over Sin

When all is well and life is good, you've probably had moments when you were less likely to sin. But these times are not the norm. What about when you have a bad day? What about when you experience a serious trial or a crisis? Do you second-guess what is right and what is wrong? Do you fall away from God's heart and His plan for you?

Here's something you should never forget: Throughout His earthly existence—including His final days—Jesus committed no sin! He experienced betrayal, lying, and brutality on the way to the cross. And still He did not sin. You have the power of Jesus on your side and over your sin when you face a trial, no matter how difficult it seems. You have the strength of the Holy Spirit in you to enable you to walk through difficult situations without giving in to sin.

Lord, I praise You and thank You for not leaving me to fight sin on my own. Through Your sacrifice I can rest in the power of the Holy Spirit when I walk through trials, tough times, and lonely days. Amen.

A PERSONAL NOTE FROM

Elizabeth

I have a saying that helps me with my prayer life: First things first. I make my quiet time with God the first thing I do each morning. This makes a tremendous difference in my day. It reminds me who I am (God's child) and who I am to serve (Him!) and what I am to do with my day…and my life (glorify Him). The very act of prayer changes my heart toward others. God gives me His love and His wisdom for living out relationships in a way that causes Christ to shine through me.

And now I have a question for you: Do you think praying—even for just five or ten minutes a day—can change your life? I know it can! Hanging out in God's presence will increase your faith, provide a place for you to unload your burdens, remind you that God is always near, and help you not to panic when troubles come. When you accept God's invitation to pray, He'll change your heart and life.

All this…and more!…is available to you, my friend, as you nurture a heart devoted to prayer. What will your first step be?

In Him,

Elizabeth

Full Access

Do you realize that, like Jesus, you can call upon God to help you make the right choices in life? Do you know you can experience victory over sin? You can choose to say no to doing wrong. Sure, your choices may require you to do it, take it, or don't do it, whatever the specific case may be. Scottish devotional writer Thomas Guthrie warned, "Never fear to suffer; but oh! fear to sin. If you must choose between them, prefer the greatest suffering to the smallest sin." The world takes ungodliness very lightly for the most part. Yet as a follower of Christ, you should resist sin even more than you avoid suffering. That's a new way to think about it, isn't it?

Can you make this the perspective of your heart too? When you turn to God for help, He will help you choose not to sin. Don't miss out on your full access to the same Source of help Jesus had. Your God is amazing, and He's right here for you.

God, I can't believe I have the privilege of asking for Your help just as Jesus did. Wow! I read in the Bible how much Christ relied on prayer and Your leading. May I do the same today. Amen.

Follow the Leader

Were you good at the children's game "Follow the Leader"? Did you follow instructions and mimic the steps of whoever was in charge? Gentleness means following Jesus' example without complaining, without resisting, without arguing. God wants to protect and care for you as you follow Him unquestioningly. Don't you want to be easy to work with and be with? Be in sync with God! Breathe a huge sigh of relief and hand over to God any part of your life that you haven't given to Him.

Jesus said in Matthew 11:29, "Take my yoke upon you and learn from me, for I am gentle and humble in heart." Do you want to follow Jesus' example of gentleness? Then commit your way to Him. Jesus' gentleness was grounded in complete trust in His loving Father. And yours can be too as you follow Jesus' lead in every step you take.

Jesus, I want my heart and my life to mirror Your heart and purpose. When I want to follow my own path, remind me that it doesn't lead to the life You have for me. Amen.

Are You Like Jesus?

You love Jesus. You study Him and His teachings in the Bible. You pray to Him. So are you growing to be like Him? You might think *How can I be like Jesus? I'm always making mistakes!* To walk with Christ and strive to be like Him is your Christian adventure! To embrace this mission, spend time reflecting on your life. Pray about your conduct and lifestyle as you consider your Savior and your call to follow His example. Do any glaring areas of sin leap to your mind and heart? Confess them now. Then determine what you will do to deal with them and eliminate them! In 1 John 1:9 the Bible says, "If we confess our sins, [Jesus] is faithful and just and will forgive us our sins and purify us from all unrighteousness." Isn't it wonderful that you have forgiveness in Jesus? His mercy and love draw you closer to His heart each day. And closer to His example!

Heavenly Father, forgive me for my sins. Help me become more Christlike in my heart and in my life. I will come to You with my prayers for repentance. I want to be like Jesus! Amen.

Amazing Conversation

Have the best conversation of your life with the best friend in your life. As you grow in prayer, and as prayer becomes more and more a part of your life, you'll find God becoming your closest friend. You'll discover that He can help you with everything important in your life right now and always—your family, your friends, your school, and your dreams for the future.

Through prayer you worship God, express your love for Him, and bring your needs before Him. And just wait and see how He answers! These will be the most incredible conversations *of* your life *for* your life. What an amazing privilege to talk one-on-one and straight from the heart with the God of the universe!

Lord, I know You really hear me. I know You know me deeply, personally, and fully. I love being known like that. I trust You and sense Your love for me. Thank You for always listening to my heart. Amen.

Watch Out!

When you're approaching a dangerous curve in the road or a rocky shoulder along a highway, yellow signs alert you to immediate risk. Sometimes flashing lights warn you to be careful. Caution! When you're approaching the most dangerous attitude of the heart—rebellion—there are also warning signs. Whether you're living in bold resistance to God's truth or practicing quiet rebellion by doing things your own way, God's Word presents a blinking beacon through its stories of disobedience, faithlessness, and wrong choices. Sometimes you'll find a reflection of your rebellious heart. But you'll also discover God's love for His children, His compassion, His forgiveness, His judgment, and His correction.

In the Bible, God helps you find your way by alerting you to dangerous behavior. And God straightens your crooked path by making all you need to be faithful available through His grace.

Jesus, I know I have a rebellious heart at times. Examples in the Bible remind me of my desire to be in charge of my own path. Help me pay attention to Your words of caution and direction. Lead me, Lord. Amen.

Birthday Present of Prayer

On my tenth birthday in the Lord I prayed and thanked God for His mercy, grace, wisdom, and salvation. And then I prayed, "Lord, is there anything missing from my Christian life that I should focus on for the next ten years?" Right away I knew in my heart what the answer was. It was prayer! I "heard" God's call to prayer in my heart. That day I opened up a special blank book my daughter Katherine had given me and wrote, "I dedicate and purpose to spend the next ten years in the Lord developing a meaningful prayer life."

Whether this is your four-month or your five-year anniversary in the Lord, ask Him what He wants you to focus on in the days, weeks, and years ahead. Spend time praying for direction. Give yourself the gift of God's direction.

God, what is missing from my Christian life?
What should I focus on in my devotional time
and in my walk with You? Show me, Lord. I'm
excited to celebrate many birthdays in You. Amen.

Live It Out!

With God's Word as your guide, you'll discover each fruit of the Spirit and how it can be cultivated as you walk with God. Savor love, joy, peace, patience, kindness, goodness, faithfulness, gentleness, and self-control as each one is made real in your life. Let God's fruit shape you, your faith, your relationship with Him, and your character. Take God's message with you into your daily life. Get your act together, get along with everybody, get the right attitudes, get it all going, and get the most out of your life.

It's one thing to talk about spiritual fruit, but God wants you to live it out. He wants you to walk the walk! Study the Bible to discover what He wants your life to look like and what He wants others to see in you.

God, You give me a game plan for my life and the fruit of the Spirit I need to carry out that plan and purpose. I want to give You my walk, my words, my actions, my praise, and my devotion. Amen.

Talk, Talk, Talk

Talk...and more talk! Oh, how people love to talk about prayer! But it's quite another thing to actually pray, isn't it? It can be tough to make the time, develop the habit, and stay with prayer instead of letting your mind wander. There is one great, surefire way to get started: Jump into prayer! Put your book down (after finishing this page!), grab a kitchen timer, and go somewhere where you can shut the door or be alone. Then pray for five minutes. Use these five golden minutes to pour out your heart's desire to your heavenly Father. Tell Him how much you love Him. And tell Him how much you long to answer His call upon your life to become—and be!—a woman of prayer.

Next round, set the timer for 10 minutes, then 20. Soon you'll be longing for more and more time with your friend Jesus.

Okay, God, let's talk! I've been missing out on the chance to talk to You for too long. I have so much to share with You and so much to ask. I love You! Amen.

THE HEART OF THE MATTER

God's Word on Faithfulness

1. Read Matthew 25:14-30, Jesus' parable of the talents. What words did Jesus use to praise those who are reliable?

2. What words did He use regarding those who are not faithful?

3. What do you find most encouraging from Jesus' story and teaching on faithfulness? Why?

4. Read 1 Timothy 3:11 and list the four qualities required in a woman who serves in her church.

   -
   -
   -
   -

5. Why do you think faithfulness is one of the qualifications for service to others in a church?

6. Read the following verses in your Bible and note how each instructs you regarding faithfulness and encourages you to be faithful.

Psalm 138:3 —

Proverbs 31:27 —

Luke 16:10 —

1 Corinthians 9:27 —

Philippians 4:13 —

Christopher Robin Prayers

A lot of Christians pray "Christopher Robin" prayers. He's the boy who struggled with his evening prayers. Little Christopher became so distracted by everything that he couldn't remember who or what to pray for. He ended up praying "God bless _____" prayers, filling in the blank with names of his family and friends.

Can you relate? Do you run out of things to pray? Does your mind wander? Do you become shy and self-conscious as soon as you enter God's presence? Being a woman of prayer is a daily challenge and an ongoing opportunity to grow. If you don't know who or what to pray for, it's okay to say, "God bless me and my family and my friends today." But don't settle for this short version for long. Why fill in a wimpy blank when God wants to *fulfill* your purpose, dreams, hopes, and heartfelt needs?

God, even when I'm tired, I want to
share what's going on at home and school.
I want to ask You things I don't even ask my best
friend. And I want my heart to be filled with
Your love, wisdom, and peace. Amen.

What Goes In Comes Out

Think about it. Practically speaking, nothing going in equals nothing going out. When you don't read God's Word and expose yourself to its purity and power, you probably don't think about God much and, therefore, probably don't pray a lot. Also, trivia going in equals trivia going out. When you hear a person talk trivia (about the latest TV talk show, movie news, gossip), you know what they are feeding on. Focus on quality! God's Word going in equals God's Word going out. Nothing beats that!

What are you bringing into your life? What are you using to fill the voids in your soul and heart? It is so important to realize what your source is for truth and energy and value. Don't sell yourself short. Always go to God's Word and His truth and His love as the ultimate truth for all you need!

Jesus, You are all I need and want. Let my heart seek You as my source of strength. May my life reflect my love for You. I want what comes out of me to speak of faith, truth, and You. Amen.

Royally Committed

Prayer is truly the queen of all the habits you could desire as a woman of God. There is a great reward for time spent in prayer and developing a heart of prayer: a life of contentment in the Lord. And the beautiful miracle is that a holy and happy life can be yours each day… as you answer God's call to pray. So let the outpourings of your heart begin today!

Now, how will you commit successfully to pray? Here are some suggestions:

- Set a schedule to pray.
- Make an agreement with a friend to pray each day.
- Become part of a prayer team or prayer chain through your church.
- Step forward and embrace this royal habit.

The King of kings is waiting.

Lord, Your name is above every name.
I will enter Your presence with respect,
faithfulness, and loyalty. I will bow at Your feet
and pour out my heart and soul. Amen.

Home First

There are many ways to show concern and demonstrate a heart of love when it comes to your family. As you develop a heart that loves no matter what, especially a heart that loves those in your family circle, you'll find yourself respecting, serving, helping, and encouraging others. You'll become eager to share Jesus with everyone and pray for those in your life. Do you see how much life will change? This is big! You will change from the inside out. It's tough to show love to your family all the time. Parents and siblings get on your nerves sometimes. But don't worry—God is *always* with you. He sees what you deal with, and He'll give you a new way of thinking, being, and loving.

Put on a heart that loves. Make loving those in your family your first priority.

God, sometimes I'm nicer to my friends than to my own family. I get so frustrated. But when I trust Your unending power and Your love instead of relying on my own limited supply, I know I'll do better. Amen.

The Foolish and Trivial

Whenever you become consumed with what is foolish and trivial, you'll fail to pray. It's a given! And then what happens? The difference between good and evil and between what is wise and foolish becomes a little fuzzy. And then what happens? You lose sight of the primary thing in life—your relationship with God! People tend to spend their very limited and priceless time and energy on things so much less important than God's kingdom and His righteousness. But, praise God, the opposite is true when you pray! He helps you direct your energy, efforts, and time toward what truly matters in the big picture of life—living life as He means for you to do it.

Commit your life to what really counts. Direct your life toward the eternal, not the earthly. That's what the wise woman does—and it's done through prayer.

Jesus, turn my foolish thoughts upside down and inside out. Banish them! Give me Your wisdom each day. I want to always know the difference between what is eternal and temporary. Amen.

He's Waiting

You can talk all day long with people you know really well, but how do you do when talking to someone you just met? Even five minutes can seem like a lifetime. You run out of topics. You get bored. You look for something better to do because you don't have a connection. Sometimes the same thing happens in your visits with God. When you stay away from an active prayer life, God can seem far away. At least far from your thoughts. You might even feel awkward when you first return to prayer. But when you begin talking to God daily, you come near to Him and get connected.

If you're putting off talking to God, don't do it any longer! He hasn't changed, disappeared, or withdrawn His love for you. And He hasn't stopped listening to you. No, if there's a problem with distance…the distance is on your side. So draw close to God. He's waiting for you.

Lord, I'm so thankful that You patiently wait for me to return to Your presence. I'm sorry for the times I wander away and become distant. I'm here today to close the gap for good. Amen.

Looking Out for You

The God of creation is looking out for *you.* Your life. Your spiritual health. Your purpose. Your needs. Your friends. Your family. Your heart. It's tough to fully understand God's goodness and His desire and ability to provide more for you than you could ever hope for or imagine. Thankfully you can go straight to the Source and ask questions and bring your requests before Him. Answer God's call to pray! Ask boldly and passionately for the salvation of your family and friends. Ask earnestly to know God's will. Ask for your daily needs at home, at school, at your job, and with your friends.

Cultivate the childlike faith of the little boy who, ready for bed, came in to announce to his family in the living room, "I'm going to say my prayers now. Anybody want anything?" God is looking out for you. Are you looking *to* God for every need?

Lord, when I'm wondering if anyone notices who I am and what I need, You are right here— knowing me, seeing me, caring for me. May I start looking to You every day. I want to bring my every need and hope to You. Amen.

Elizabeth

God gave two kings opportunities to lead Israel, but in the end they went down different paths. Saul walked away from God, and David walked toward Him. These two men were like two musicians, one who sits down at a piano and plunks on it now and then and the other who plays for hours and is a disciplined student. The first creates uncertain sounds that fade away, while the other excels and lifts the hearts of others as he fine-tunes his music. Saul's song—his walk with the Lord—was on again, off again, and undeveloped. But David, known as "the sweet psalmist of Israel," offered up to God pure melodies of devoted love and heartfelt obedience.

Is yours a heart of obedience? God tells you and me to "guard" our hearts with all diligence, for it affects everything we do. He tells us to look straight ahead and not get sidetracked. The key to living a life that stays on God's path is your heart—a heart after God.

In Him,

Elizabeth

Out from Under a Secret

Do you avoid talking to your parents when you've done something against their wishes? Do you do the same with God? You're not alone. Adam and Eve hid themselves from God after they sinned. King David ceased praying and "kept silent" after he sinned. Hiding your secrets behind silence keeps you trapped in those sins. Don't deny your errors, blame others for them, hide them, or excuse them. Own up to your wrongs and go to God for forgiveness! Never lose your ability and your opportunity to pray for yourself and others because of being too proud or stubborn to deal with sin. Too much is at stake to hold on to secret or "favorite" sins.

The prayers of a godly woman—the one who seeks to walk in obedience, who confesses and forsakes her offenses before God—bring powerful results. Don't hide behind sin and miss out on the powerful forgiveness of Christ and the sweet talks with Him that follow.

God, forgive me for staying quiet when I have so much to confess and share. I take ownership for my sin today and ask for Your forgiveness. I want to keep our dialog going all the days of my life. Amen.

You're Saying Something!

When you're not talking to God, you're still saying something. Maybe you're saying, "I don't believe in the power of prayer, so why bother?" Maybe your silence says, "I don't need God. I can take care of myself, thank You!" Or maybe you don't pray because you don't know how. Even those closest to Jesus—His disciples—had the same problem. They watched Jesus pray. They heard Jesus pray. They even heard Jesus pray for them! Finally, as recorded in Luke 11:1, they went to the Master Pray-er Himself and asked, "Lord, teach us to pray." Pray this same prayer for yourself.

Take the first step and start praying...and keep praying, even when you don't feel like it, even when you think it doesn't make any difference, even if you don't know what you're doing or fear you're doing it badly. Pray!

Jesus, teach me to pray. Help me open up and express all of me and my life. When I'm doubting or afraid free me from these obstacles. Amen.

Making Space for God

Are you making room for your devotional time? Not physical space necessarily, but a place in your life. If you've tried to schedule a time but it didn't stick, try this plan: As soon as dinner is over get ready for bed. Really. Finish homework, wash your face, brush your teeth, create a "to-do" list for the next day, and get into your pj's. Then set out your prayer notebook and Bible in a place where you'll have devotions the next morning—a desk, a window seat, a favorite chair with a side table. Early to bed, early to rise…so you can meet with God for a pre-breakfast date.

My principle is that "something is better than nothing." If your morning devotional time with God is only five minutes at first, that's fine. In time, as you begin to taste the fruits of time spent in prayer, you'll go to greater lengths to give even more space to time with God.

Jesus, I'll meet You in the morning each day this month. Give me a sense of priority in the evening so I will prepare for my pre-breakfast devotional date with You. I want to create a lifelong habit starting today! Amen.

Eyes to Jesus

Look around. What...or who...influences you? Are you influenced positively for the things of God? Are you overcome with a desire for "things" when you see a model on the cover of a magazine wearing the latest fashion? Even if there are good articles, the overall messages can be the exact opposite of the messages God's Word sends to your heart. You can become so captivated by the world's offerings that you lose sight of God's better offer. The more you read the Bible and pray, the more clearly you'll see the difference between the diet of worldliness and the diet of godliness.

How can you "turn your eyes upon Jesus" so that the things of this world will fade to the background? Identify three things you can do today to turn your heart toward spiritual things—toward God.

-
-
-

Jesus, my eyes are upon You. When my gaze turns toward the world's version of life or greatness or love, remind me of Your unchanging love for me. Amen.

Don't Lose It

The Bible shares a story of two sisters named Martha and Mary that reveals the need to set priorities. You can read about them in Luke 10:38-42. In a nutshell, Martha was a very busy woman who did a lot of good things…but carried them to such an extreme that she "lost it" on the glorious day when Jesus came to visit. She fell apart when her sister stopped her kitchen work to go sit at the feet of Jesus.

Both sisters loved Jesus, and both gladly served Him. But Mary knew when to stop with the busyness and do the best thing, the one thing that's most important—spend time with God. And you can do the same. Don't lose your sanity by stressing. God calls You to come to Him instead!

Lord, sometimes the pressures of school and home and responsibilities consume me. The stress makes me forget what really matters—being in Your presence! When I "lose it," help me find You. Amen.

The Four Presents of Peace

Don't you love receiving gifts? Here are four gifts… four sources for God's peace. Unwrap them one by one.

God, the Son. Jesus' work on the cross paved the way for your personal relationship and peace with God.

God, the Father. Through the Bible you can learn all about God, His promises, and His faithfulness so you will know you can trust Him in your times of need.

God's Word. When you follow God's Word and its teachings, you experience the peace that comes with keeping a right relationship with God.

God, the Spirit. John 14:27 reveals what the gift of the Holy Spirit is: "Peace I leave with you; my peace I give you. I do not give as the world gives. Do not let your heart be troubled and do not be afraid." The Holy Spirit guides you to peace.

Doesn't this make you want to pause and give thanks to God for these four gifts? Do it right now!

God, I am so grateful for Your peace.
On my own I stumble, I avoid challenges,
and I've even given up. The peace I find through
You, Jesus, the Holy Spirit, and Your Word
changes my worry to worship. Amen.

On a Plan and a Prayer

Pay close attention to James 1:2: "Consider it pure joy, my brothers, whenever you face trials of many kinds." Did you catch that? James did not say *if*...but *whenever* you face trials. You will encounter difficulties, struggles, heartaches, and disappointments. Faith in God doesn't eliminate trials, but it does give you a person to go to with them. You can create a plan for dealing with trouble—God's way. What scriptures will you use to stay strong in the Lord as you walk through painful trials? And what, when, and how will you pray about the troubles of life—past, present, and future?

If you're still wondering, *With all these troubles, what's the difference between my life of faith and that of someone without faith?* Well, did you catch the other surprise from James? "Consider it pure joy" when you face those trials. Consider it pure joy that you can depend on God for help, for guidance, for wisdom, and for comfort in those trials.

Lord, I used to try to dig myself out of situations rather than call to You for help. Help me stick to my plan of faith to turn to You always. Amen.

THE HEART OF THE MATTER

God's Word on Gentleness

1. What does God command in the following verses?

   Galatians 6:1—

   Ephesians 4:2—

   Colossians 3:12—

   1 Timothy 6:11—

   2 Timothy 2:24-25—

   Titus 3:1-2—

2. Why is gentleness so important to God?

3. Why is gentleness important to your walk with God?

4. Consider these examples from the Bible of some who learned what it meant to "take it," to look to God for His gentleness in their trying situations. Write down how these examples will help you in your life.

   The apostles (Acts 5:40-41)—

   Stephen (Acts 7:54-60)—

   Paul and Silas (Acts 16:22-25)—

   Servants to both good and harsh masters (1 Peter 2:18-21)—

Get Spiritually Involved

When you genuinely care about people, you pay attention to their circumstances and are concerned about their welfare. You get involved in their lives. As your love grows, the details of their lives become more and more important to you. It matters to you if they are sad, discouraged, struggling, or lonely. God asks you to care for everyone, even—if not especially for—those people who bother you most.

If you follow Jesus' instruction in Luke 6:28 to "pray for those who mistreat you," radical changes occur in your heart. For starters, prayer causes you to care about those you pray for. God changes your heart and mind by softening your harshness, melting your selfishness, and mellowing your judgmental spirit. As you cultivate a kind, caring heart and become spiritually involved in the lives of others, you'll begin to understand God's love for you and them on a more personal level.

Jesus, soften my heart. I pray that You will turn my attention to others. I want to genuinely care about them and their lives. Give me sensitivity and tenderness so I can look beyond me to the person standing in front of me. Amen.

Attitude Check

When you would love to be doing something else—like hanging out with friends—but you need to go to practice, finish your schoolwork, help your parents around the house, or watch your younger brother or sister, pray to be faithful and trustworthy. Instead of grumbling about what you can't do, embrace what you're given to do. Every moment of your day is an offering to the Lord. When your attitude is smudged with resentment, anger, jealousy, stubbornness, or disappointment, you're making the moment all about you. You're ignoring God, others, and your purpose each time this happens. Don't let your attitude ruin what God plans for you to learn, discover, and honor in every moment.

Set aside your negative attitude. Pray for a joyful spirit and patience with obstacles or people-problems that come up during your day. And pray for self-control so emotions don't spill out and hurt someone else or interfere with God's plan.

Jesus, forgive me when I lose control of my emotions. I become blind to my chances to help, reach out, or be faithful to Your leading when I'm thinking just of me. May Your joy replace my anger. Amen.

Get into the Habit

When you're in the habit of praying, you're more likely to think of asking for God's help first instead of later or last, when all else fails. So I pray God's message to your heart is crystal clear. When you're in trouble... pray! When you're helpless...pray! When you've done all you can do but you're still in need of help...pray! When you encounter an only-God-can-meet-it need... pray! When you have a specific need...pray! Prayer is God's avenue for you. He calls you to pray whenever something—anything!—is important to you. So in times of trouble and need...pray!

Now, what can you do to improve your prayer life? How will that make a difference? And when can you get started? Put it on your personal prayer list, ask another person to check on you, and then go to work on kicking your prayer habit up a notch!

Lord, Your message is clear. You want me to come to You with everything. You created prayer so that I can connect with You and carry Your wisdom into my days. Help me grow my prayer life. Amen.

When Friendships Fade

Have you ever had a friendship that started out great, but then something went wrong? The other person made a new friend and became "too busy." Maybe your friend said something about you that wasn't true or that hurt your feelings. Maybe she turned against you. Maybe she walked away from your special friendship… and joined a clique. Maybe she let you down when you were really counting on her help. And in the end you were left wondering, "What happened?"

You don't head into a relationship expecting to be hurt. When a friendship fades, you feel confused and discouraged. What are you to do with your broken heart? As always, God comes to your rescue. Bring your hurt feelings, wounds of the heart, and fears about future friendships to Him in prayer. He'll mend you because His love for you is constant and shines brightly.

God, it's hard to be friendly and open with others now that I've been hurt by a friend. Please help me move on and draw strength and courage from my relationship with You. Amen.

Relationship Advice

It can be easy to pout, hold a grudge, or allow bitterness to take root in your heart when people disappoint you. Have you refused to talk to someone who failed you? Or resorted to gossip to get back at a friend? Go straight to God's Word for relationship advice. He has wisdom for you in Ephesians 4:32: Forgive each other just as in Christ God forgave you. Jesus models the right way of dealing with those who disappoint you. He says to pray for them.

God's servant Samuel spent his life teaching God's people. But the day came when they rejected him. In the book of 1 Samuel we read that God told him to speak to the people about their sin. Wouldn't that be the last thing you would want to do? But Samuel obeyed, and those who betrayed him were ashamed and begged him to pray for them. Did he snub them? No, Samuel forgave God's people...and prayed for them. His obedience allowed the relationship to be restored.

Lord, release me from a bitter heart so
I can still serve You and even those who have hurt
me. Give me Your perspective so I can help restore,
not ruin relationships. Amen.

A Helping Hand

Are you familiar with the fable that tells of a man who is crying for help while he is drowning in a river? Meanwhile, on the bridge above, another man is leaning over the rail looking at the struggling man. The observer tells the drowning man what he should have done and lets him know what he should do if he ever falls into the water again. Instead of reaching in with a helping hand and saving the dying man's life, he talks... and talks. The perishing man didn't need a lecture. He needed someone to save him!

When it comes to praying for those who have fallen and failed, stop with the lectures, put aside judgment, and go to work helping them. Correction and instruction may come later, but when someone is in trouble—pray...and offer a helping hand!

Lord, when I want to talk at someone who is facing a struggle, remind me that he or she first needs help! And when I'm facing trials, may I reach out to You as my primary source of help. Amen.

God's Way Out

When you find yourself in trouble do you wish for a driver's license and a car to drive a few states away? A plane to go an even greater distance? Or at least a hideout where you can go for rest and shelter? As hard as it can be, you must stay and fight your battle with prayer, prayer, prayer! And be assured, if "a way out" becomes necessary, if the heat of battle or the burden becomes more than you can bear, "God is faithful." So faithful that in 1 Corinthians 10:13 He promises He will provide an escape route. And God's way out will be a better plan than anything you could come up with! He will deliver you. He will come to your aid. He will rescue you. You can depend on Him. As David declared in Psalm 55:16-17, "I call to God, and the LORD saves me....I cry out in distress, and he hears my voice."

God, hear my cry! I feel cornered by my circumstances and the desire to flee is overwhelming. Instead, I will hold tightly to Your faithfulness. I will pray, wait, and watch for Your way through this. Amen.

See What God Will Do

God is a master chef. He can make sweet what is bitter...even when it is your heart. He is a Counselor. He makes the one who is sad become glad. And He is your Redeemer. He turns something bad into something good. Oh, please, don't wish your hard times away. Some of your most meaningful times with God will come when you talk to Him about your hurts.

Now, what's troubling you? As you face your challenge, talk to your almighty, all-powerful, miracle-working, mountain-moving God. Don't just stand there. Don't cave in. Don't worry. And don't suffer. As James 5:13 asks, "Is any one among you in trouble? He should pray." See what God will do with this trial before you. It will be amazing!

Lord, You are my Savior. You can turn my weaknesses into strengths. You can make my present trial a pathway to Your joy. Transform my pain into purpose. Turn my loss into hope. Amen.

A PERSONAL NOTE FROM

Elizabeth

If I could wish one thing for you, if I could have one prayer answered for you, it would be this: I would pray that you begin today to go through life as a giver. You see, the world seems to be divided into two kinds of people—those who give and those who take. The giver is other-oriented and the taker is self-oriented. Those who think of others are Christlike, and those who think only of themselves tend to lie and manipulate. Their hearts are set on themselves and not on Christ or on others.

I want you to be a giver! I want you to make a difference in the lives of other people. I want you to join with me in my goal to better the life of every person God allows to cross my path. I don't want you to suffer and flop around like I did before I knew God. I want you to know what God's great plan is for your life as His woman. My vision for you is large. It's grand! There is so much God desires for you. And I desire it too!

In Him,

Elizabeth

Always with You

What's the secret of always having peace? Knowing that your heavenly Father is always with you! God is omnipresent—everywhere at once—and fully aware of every detail of your life. He knows your needs at all times and in every situation. In Psalm 139:7-10 David declared, "If I go up to the heavens, you are there; if I make my bed in the depths, you are there...if I settle on the far side of the sea, even there your hand will guide me."

Imagine it! You can never be any place—from the heights of heaven to the depths of the sea and everywhere in between—where God is not present and available to you. Do you see? The key to peace is not the absence of problems. No, it's the *presence of God*. Wow! Let that truth wash over you for a minute.

God, You are with me no matter where I go or what I'm doing. When I'm sad or feeling lonely and distant from people around me, You are right here with Your peace and comfort. I need You. Thank You for loving me and being here for me. Amen.

Let It Flow

How encouraging to know that as a believer you are not left on your own to cope with life's problems. Even when you don't know the right words to pray, the Holy Spirit does. He prays with you and for you.

Here's a secret. Let the prayers of your heart flow. When you are in pain…pray. When you are speechless…pray. When you are heartsick…pray. When you are suffering, beaten up, or beaten down by life…pray. When you are troubled or perplexed…pray. When you are overwhelmed…pray.

Your heavenly Father knows what you need *before* you ask. Isn't that incredible? So don't be afraid to bring up anything and everything. God wants to hear from you. Use any words or cries you can muster in your hurting heart. Just be sure you pray…and leave the rest to God.

God, You know what I'm going to say before I do! It gives me peace to know You have such knowledge of me and still love me. I won't stress today. I'm ready to let my prayers flow to You. Amen.

How Can I Know?

You probably struggle with the same question women of any age struggle with, "How can I possibly know which things are God's will and which aren't?" God doesn't leave you hanging when it comes to "gray" areas of daily life. He gives you a conscience. It helps you to know when to move ahead in full faith…and when to hold back.

If you're not sure an action is right or wrong, then you shouldn't do it. If you do something you're not sure about, doubt sets in and your confidence weakens. As a Christian, be confident your actions and decisions are right and godly before acting. This adds unbelievable power to your life. Instead of waffling and wondering, you can act decisively and worry free. Hold off on any commitment until after prayer, which includes listening for God's response. Wait for clear direction, a clear conscience, and the absence of doubt and guilt. This is the life of faith and confidence!

Lord, I want to move forward in full faith.
I'm not always confident at school or at home,
but I know I can act with confidence and
assurance in You and Your leading. Amen.

Most Important Day

What is the most important day ever? Are you thinking of your birthday? The day you were baptized? Those are very significant days. But the most important day for applying God's Word and following His will is *today*. Jesus told us not to wait, think, or wonder about tomorrow. Matthew 6:34 records His words, "Do not worry about tomorrow, for tomorrow will worry about itself. Each day has enough trouble of its own." Today has enough demands, quirks, and surprises to use up all of your effort and strength. So focus on God's wisdom. You will be called upon to walk and act with wisdom and according to God's will all day long…around every corner and in every encounter.

So how was your yesterday? And how is your today going? Be sure to pray yourself through each day!

God, help me honor today—the most important day—by following Your wisdom. When worries of tomorrow take over my thoughts, give me Your peace so I can focus on the gifts and needs of today. Amen.

Watch Out for that Curveball!

Life throws curveballs now and then. There's no avoiding them. But you can smack them with God's wisdom! Wisdom sees life from God's perspective. What is God's perspective? Here are a few observations from Proverbs about the *opposite* of wisdom.

The fool envies the wealthy. The fool scorns his elders. The fool does not ask advice. The fool hates his neighbor. The fool sleeps his life away. The fool squanders his money. The fool despises wisdom. The fool speaks slander. The fool lies. The fool talks too much. The fool argues and quarrels.

Are you seeing and living life from the opposite of these—from God's perspective? Prayer makes the difference! Close your eyes in prayer and in tune to God's way of seeing things. And be prepared for the unexpected.

God, You protect me from foolish and hurtful behaviors, decisions, and actions. I want to listen to You more. I will study Your wisdom and pray for Your direction. Set me apart for You. Amen.

The Source!

There's a lot of advice and information everywhere you turn. But wisdom is much more scarce. You have an advantage over many people because you have an endless source of wisdom in God and His Word. Connect with wisdom by praying, "Lord, Your Word says in James 1:5, 'If any of you lacks wisdom, he should ask God...and it will be given to him.' So here I am! I need wisdom, and I'm asking You for it. Please reveal Your wisdom in this matter."

Look up Proverbs 3:5 and 6 and pray, "And, Lord, Your Word also says to 'trust in the LORD with all your heart and lean not on your own understanding; in all your ways acknowledge him, and he will make your paths straight.' I don't want to rely on my own heart, so I'm asking You right now, Lord, to guide my footsteps. What is the right thing to do here? What is the right decision? What is the path You want me to walk in?"

Lord, when I get caught up in lies or ignorance or the world's standards for living, fill my mind and heart with Your knowledge. I love that I can always go to You—the Source of true wisdom. Amen.

Questions Before the Answers

It's hard to explain how, but when you pray and wait for God's answer, you receive direction and confidence from Him! He impresses His will on your heart. When you have decisions to make, take this heart quiz:

Question 1: Why would I do this?—What would your motives for doing this particular thing be?

Question 2: Why would I not do this?—Base this on what you know to be right or wrong according to the Bible. Is your answer all about fear, laziness, or indifference? If so, pray over that area.

Question 3: Why should I do this?—As you pray, God will lead you to the answer that is right.

Question 4: Why should I not do this?—Read Proverbs 12:15: "The way of a fool seems right to him, but a wise man listens to advice."

God, when I'm honest about my reasons for doing something or not doing something, I am better able to receive Your will. Lead me toward truth and honesty. I want to be wise in You. Amen.

So Much Life in a Life!

A life of faith, a life of wisdom, and a life of understanding all unfold when you pray. Why wait to have all this? Start by putting every activity and possibility on trial through prayer. There are plenty of activities that will compete for your time and energy. Which ones should you accept? Ask God for His wisdom as you choose your activities carefully and intelligently. And ask your parents or pastor for their input. God works through them too! What fabulous confidence you'll have in your heart as you walk in God's will. When you answer God's call to pray, you become the woman He designed you to be, one who walks with Him in faith, wisdom, understanding, and confidence.

Can you remember a decision you made without help or guidance from God or others? What happened? What would you do differently now, and why? Say yes to the right activities, and you'll enjoy a life filled with purpose.

God, help me make good, better, and best decisions. I want Your confidence to shine in my life. Thank You for giving me plenty of activities. I'm glad I can call on You any time for help. Amen.

THE HEART OF THE MATTER

God's Word on Self-Control

1. Look at these scriptures in your Bible and note God's message to you about self-control.

   Romans 6:12—

   Galatians 5:16—

   Romans 6:13—

   1 Corinthians 10:31—

   Galatians 5:24—

2. In what areas of your life do you struggle the most with self-control?

3. What lessons do you learn from these people about self-control or the lack of self-control?

   Joseph and Potiphar's wife (Genesis 39:7-10)—

   Moses (Numbers 20:2-11)—

   Achan (Joshua 7:21)—

   David (1 Samuel 24:3-7 and 26:7-9)—

   David (1 Samuel 24:8-15 and 26:10)—

   David (2 Samuel 11:1-4)—

Look at Him

When you pray out loud in a group your words, attitude, and heart should all be saying, "Look at Him!" Jesus cautions not to use prayer as a means of getting attention. Have you ever been around someone who seemed to pray to attract an audience? They sound like they're talking to the people in the group instead of to God. Or maybe they're going on and on in a pious sort of way.

In Matthew 6:5-6 Jesus says, "When you pray, do not be like the hypocrites, for they love to pray standing in the synagogues and on the street corners to be seen by men....But when you pray, go into your room, close the door and pray to your Father, who is unseen. Then your Father, who sees what is done in secret, will reward you." When your only desire is to worship God and praise Him and pour out your heart to Him, there is no need to be showy. Speak to your Father with respect, humility, and your sweet love.

God, I want to honor You with my prayers.
May my motives be pure when I pray in a group
or alone in my room. I want all the attention
to be on You. Amen.

All About Commitment

Are you good at keeping your commitments? Are you committed to being honest with your parents? To studying for school? To practicing and staying strong for athletics? These are all good, but there is a biggie beyond this list: Are you committed to God? Romans 12:1 says "to offer your bodies as living sacrifices, holy and pleasing to God—this is your spiritual act of worship." Begin a new practice this week of dedicating yourself to God daily. And how can you do this? One person wrote down a list of rules to live by. And what was #1 on his list? "Make a daily, definite, audible dedication of yourself to God." Say it out loud—Lord, today I give myself anew to you.

Did you do it? Say it aloud again. And again tomorrow. Why not say this commitment to God daily for a week? And then choose to make it a habit for life!

Lord, I give myself to You. I know You love me and value me because I am Your child. I give all of me to serve You, know You, and please You. Amen.

Power from the Page!

There is power in God's Word! When you go straight to the Bible, you are going straight to God's heart and power. Hebrews 4:12 says, "The word of God is living and active. Sharper than any double-edged sword." Make it a goal to use scriptures in your prayers. You don't know which scriptures to use? Try this. Highlight your favorite prayer verses in your Bible with a marker. You can even record them in the back of this book. Then pray these verses. When you draw your words directly from His truths, you honor God. Some verses will remind you of certain people and situations in your life. Again, write these down and include them in your prayer time.

Here's another great way to pray using the power of God's Word—insert people's names into different verses. Do a trial run through Colossians 1:9-10. You'll love praying for your friends and family in this exciting and easy way!

God, I love Your Word and the power it gives.
Help me search it, use it, memorize it,
and pray it with passion. Amen.

A Prayer Library

When you run out of things to say to God, don't give up. Try borrowing! Read and pray through the written prayers of others. Their powerful prayers help you grow in your passion and "prayer language" by their eloquence.

These prayers might be from Christian authors, ministers, and believers from the past. Look for books about the prayer journeys God's people have taken with Him through the centuries. Let their stories teach you and inspire you! You can also borrow and pray words from the prayers of the Bible. Psalm 92:2 calls us to declare God's "love in the morning" and His "faithfulness at night." Morning and evening prayers have been labeled by some as "dawn and dusk bookends." Develop the habit of beginning and ending each day with prayer.

Lord, when I read the powerful prayers
of Christians who have gone before me or
who influence me today, I feel the strength of
the body of Christ. Each word I lift up is
straight from my heart to Yours. Amen.

Staying Connected

Does your phone ever cut out in the middle of a conversation? It might be the phone or it might be the signal…either way it's frustrating! You want to listen to people, and you want to be heard. God provides you with a secure line that keeps you speaking clearly without any problems. It's called honesty. Have you ever told a lie? Or deliberately left something out (the lie of omission)? This is just like calling with a bad signal. The other person only hears part of the story because you cut out the truth. Lying can seem helpful by making things easier for yourself or better for the other person. But the truth you leave out is what needs to be heard.

Always tell the truth! Sometimes you'll end up in situations you didn't choose, but truthfulness keeps your connection to God and to others solid.

Lord, when a lie is about to come out of my mouth or I want to share only part of the truth, keep me quiet! Help me express myself honestly and with kindness. I want to reflect Your integrity. Amen.

Stand by Your Choice

When you finally make the decision to pray over each decision...stick with it. Learn to honor yourself and your commitments as you honor God. If you have made promises to give every choice over to God...and failed, never fear...today is your chance to begin again and create a pact with God.

One way to follow through is to give your first decision each day to God. Pray. Don't start thinking about school or what you'll have for breakfast or what you'll wear. Begin with prayer. This choice provides the time and opportunity to pray over your decisions. God will lead you to find and fulfill His will for your time, your day, and your life. Once time is spent making decisions in prayer, your time is better managed, spent, and saved as a result of walking in God's will. Prayer is so powerful. Give each decision, choice, path, possibility, worry, and want over to His care.

God, I want to give to You my day, my heart,
my decisions. May I begin each morning with
thoughts of You and Your will for me.
I want to follow Your ways and give to You every
part of myself and my life. Amen.

What's Goin' On?

What's going on in your life these days? Are you too busy? Are you taking it too easy? Think through your routine. Are you making time for God? On your calendar, write down the exact time you'll pray each day for the next week. Be sure to keep these appointments just like you keep your dates with your friends. As one of my prayer principles says, "There is no right or wrong way to pray...except not to pray!" Shade in each calendar day that you keep your commitment.

What do you dream will be true of your "Prayer Calendar" over the course of a month or two? Will there be more shaded squares than blank ones? What can you do today to make your prayer dream a reality?

Lord, I've got my prayer dates written down on my calendar and on my heart and mind. I look forward to meeting You here each day to talk things over. May I be faithful in this commitment. Amen.

A PERSONAL NOTE FROM

Elizabeth

Whew! You did it. You made it all the way to the end. Well done! Congratulations! And a big pat on the back to you! Now hopefully you will go through the book again and again to keep its truths and encouragement alive in your daily life.

But even more important than reading your book again is continuing to put what you've read to work in your heart and your walk with God. I pray that you will think about, desire, talk to God about—

- fruit that evidences His work in your heart
- character qualities that reflect His standards
- knowledge that enlarges your understanding of Him
- spiritual growth that makes you more like Jesus, and
- Joy in the Lord no matter what's happening.

In His everlasting love,
Your friend and sister in Christ,

Elizabeth

What I'm Learning

❀ ❀ ❀

_____

_____

_____

_____

_____

_____

_____

_____

_____

_____

_____

What I'm Learning

My Favorite Bible Verses

❀ ❀ ❀

_____

_____

_____

_____

_____

_____

_____

_____

_____

_____

My Favorite Bible Verses

_____

_____

_____

_____

_____

_____

_____

_____

_____

_____

_____

Keys to Becoming a Woman After God's Own Heart

❀ ❀ ❀

_____

_____

_____

_____

_____

_____

_____

_____

_____

_____

_____

Keys to Becoming a Woman After God's Own Heart

❀ ❀ ❀

_____

_____

_____

_____

_____

_____

_____

_____

_____

_____

_____

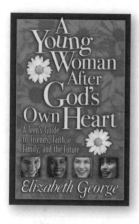

A Young Woman After God's Own Heart

Discover God's plan and purpose for your life!

What does it mean to pursue God's heart in your everyday life? It means understanding and following God's perfect plan for your friendships, your faith, your family relationships, and your future. Bible teacher Elizabeth George reveals how you can...

- grow closer to God
- enjoy meaningful relationships
- make wise choices
- become spiritually strong
- build a better future
- fulfill the desires of your heart

Get caught up in the exciting adventure of a lifetime! Become a woman after God's own heart!

Books by Elizabeth George

- Beautiful in God's Eyes
- Breaking the Worry Habit…Forever
- Finding God's Path Through Your Trials
- Following God with All Your Heart
- The Heart of a Woman Who Prays
- Life Management for Busy Women
- Loving God with All Your Mind
- Loving God with All Your Mind DVD and Workbook
- A Mom After God's Own Heart
- A Mom After God's Own Heart Devotional
- Moments of Grace for a Woman's Heart
- One-Minute Inspiration for Women
- Quiet Confidence for a Woman's Heart
- Raising a Daughter After God's Own Heart
- The Remarkable Women of the Bible
- Small Changes for a Better Life
- Walking With the Women of the Bible
- A Wife After God's Own Heart
- A Woman After God's Own Heart®
- A Woman After God's Own Heart® Deluxe Edition
- A Woman After God's Own Heart®— Daily Devotional
- A Woman's Daily Walk with God
- A Woman's Guide to Making Right Choices
- A Woman's High Calling
- A Woman's Walk with God
- A Woman Who Reflects the Heart of Jesus
- A Young Woman After God's Own Heart
- A Young Woman After God's Own Heart— A Devotional
- A Young Woman's Guide to Prayer
- A Young Woman's Guide to Making Right Choices

Study Guides

- Beautiful in God's Eyes Growth & Study Guide
- Finding God's Path Through Your Trials Growth & Study Guide
- Following God with All Your Heart Growth & Study Guide
- Life Management for Busy Women Growth & Study Guide
- Loving God with All Your Mind Growth & Study Guide
- Loving God with All Your Mind Interactive Workbook
- A Mom After God's Own Heart Growth & Study Guide
- The Remarkable Women of the Bible Growth & Study Guide
- Small Changes for a Better Life Growth & Study Guide
- A Wife After God's Own Heart Growth & Study Guide
- A Woman After God's Own Heart® Growth & Study Guide
- A Woman's Call to Prayer Growth & Study Guide
- A Woman's High Calling Growth & Study Guide
- A Woman Who Reflects the Heart of Jesus Growth & Study Guide

Children's Books

- A Girl After God's Own Heart
- A Girl After God's Own Heart Devotional
- God's Wisdom for Little Girls
- A Little Girl After God's Own Heart

Books by Jim George

- 10 Minutes to Knowing the Men and Women of the Bible
- The Bare Bones Bible® Handbook
- The Bare Bones Bible® for Teens
- A Boy After God's Own Heart
- A Husband After God's Own Heart
- Know Your Bible from A to Z
- A Leader After God's Own Heart
- A Man After God's Own Heart
- A Man After God's Own Heart Devotional
- The Man Who Makes a Difference
- One-Minute Insights for Men
- A Young Man After God's Own Heart
- A Young Man's Guide to Making Right Choices

Books by Jim & Elizabeth George

- A Couple After God's Own Heart
- A Couple After God's Own Heart Interactive Workbook
- God's Wisdom for Little Boys
- A Little Boy After God's Own Heart

About the Author

Elizabeth George is a bestselling author with more than 7 million books in print. She's a popular speaker at Christian women's events. Her passion is to teach the Bible in a way that changes young women's lives.

For information about Elizabeth's speaking ministry, to sign up for her mailings, or to purchase her books, visit her website:

www.ElizabethGeorge.com

Or write:

Elizabeth George
PO Box 2879
Belfair, WA 98528